CYBER SECURITY DISASTERS

HISTORY OF IT DISASTERS AND HOW TO AVOID THEM IN THE FUTURE

Matt Olivier

CONTENTS

Ch.1 History of Hacking 1980s

Kevin Mitnick

The FBI's search for Mitnick, together with his arrest, trial, and sentence, was very controversial at the time, and even now his black hat jobs are studied in colleges and universities around the world. Kevin is now an American computer security consultant, public speaker, writer, and founder of Mitnick Security Consulting, LLC, but his past was a bit dark with multiple malicious hacking episodes. He is well-known for his outstanding arrest in 1995 and following five-year prison sentence for several computer- and communications-related criminal jobs.

Kevin David Mitnick was born on August 6, 1963, which at the writing of this publication makes him a few days short of 58 years old.

Back in 1976, at the ripe age of 13, Kevin Mitnick employed a combination of social engineering and dumpster diving (literally crawling into garbage dumpsters and searching through the garbage for computer information like phone numbers, computer codes, technical information, usernames, and passwords) to circumvent the punch card system used from the Los Angeles bus program. He composed a story about a college project and subsequently persuaded a bus driver to convey to him where he could purchase his own ticket punch tool. Then he found unused bus transport slides in dumpsters next to the garage where city buses were placed and utilized his punch tool as a means to ride any bus in the greater Los Angeles metro area at no cost. This was the beginning of Kevin's use of social engineering methods which later became his main technique of procuring data, including usernames, passwords, along with modem telephone numbers.

The year 1979, when Kevin was 16, was a banner year for him since this is the year that he first got prohibited access to a computer network. He accomplished this feat with a telephone number that a buddy provided to him for the Ark. The Ark was a Digital Equipment Corporation (DEC) computer system which was used for developing their RSTS/E operating platform for PDP-X series computers. He sneaked into the Palo Alto Research Center and made duplications of his software, a crime for which he was charged and convicted of in 1988. Kevin had almost completed his three-year supervised release but just couldn't keep control of his hacking impulses. This resulted in his hacking Pacific Bell voice email computers, and a new warrant was issued for his arrest. Mitnick was on the lam and a fugitive for the next two and a half years. According to the U.S. Department of Justice (DOJ), Kevin obtained criminal admittance to numerous computer networks during his time as a fugitive. He made use of mobile phones he cloned (replicated) in order to hide his place from authorities. Mitnick intercepted and stole computer system passwords, created modifications to computer programs, browse private emails, and copied proprietary applications from a number of the nation's leading mobile phone and computer companies.

Kevin continually claimed that Markoff had telephoned him to operate collectively on a book he was writing about him.

Mitnick declined and Markoff then published his classic book showing Mitnick as a felonious pc criminal. As stated by Mitnick, "it all began with a series of posts by John Markoff on the pay of The New York Times, full of false accusations and defamation, which afterwards had been denied by the authorities. Markoff had it in for me because I refused to collaborate in his book and made the myth of Kevin Mitnick, to transform Takedown [his book] into a bestseller".

In 1994 using a flourishing mobile telephony market, Kevin Mitnick had returned to some illegal activities and was also a fugitive wanted by the FBI. He had been well recognized globally due to his various misadventures in personal crime, and his photograph had been circulated all over the world; so the authorities put the out the word requesting individuals who spotted him to contact law enforcement. It was during 1994 and 1995 that Mitnick became the focus of the largest manhunt hurled at a cybercriminal up until that time. Mitnick made the choice to attack yet another hacker and computer security expert, Tsutomu Shimomura. To make sure he wasn't disrupted, Kevin decided Christmas Day 1994 to establish his well-planned assault against Shimomura using a process called a TCP sequence prediction attack. To perform such an assault, Kevin needed to properly predict TCP sequence numbers being used involving Shimomura's net server along with his X-terminal. Due to the character of a TCP handshake, it's reasonably possible to be in a position to fake TCP sequence numbers. If successful, Kevin will have the ability to present as the sender (instead of Shimomura's web server) and initiate communication with Shimomura. To thwart the initial sender from sending additional packets, Kevin created use of SYN-Flood attacks against the actual sender. This was an irresistible assault because the 30-year-old Shimomura was a very respected Japanese security authority in his own right with a hacker/scientific personality nearly as intricate as Mitnick's. However, the significant difference between Mitnick and Shimomura was when

Shimomura uncovered security holes he reported them to the proper authorities, but Mitnick utilized them for illegal profit. Shimomura's firewall became the bane of Mitnick since it ended up listing all action that was occurring between Mitnick and his target. On the following day, December 26, Shimomura found that his strategy was compromised via Mitnick's intrusion (though he didn't know that it was Mitnick right away). By the time Mitnick completed his incursion into Shimomura's computer network, he had stolen the following items:

• Private emails
• Software used to control cell phones
• Various computer security tools

The game was now afoot (as Sherlock Holmes would say), and the hunt was on to find who'd taken his property and where the goods were stashed. In the latter part of January 1995, Shimomura's pilfered program was found on "The WELL" (Whole Earth Lectronic Link), a virtual online community based in Sausalito, California with a membership in the time of the writing of around 3,000 members. Kevin was utilizing The WELL as a base to launch attacks into Major company computer systems all over America. The WELL was founded by Stewart Brand and Larry Brilliant in 1985 and started as a dial-up bulletin board system, after becoming one of the very first dial-up ISPs in the 1990s and morphed to its current system as the Web evolved. Police at The WELL asked that Shimomura assist them in discovering exactly how Mitnick (title not known at that time) was breaching their computer programs. A short time later, Netcom also requested Shimomura for aid. Shimomura started working at The WELL on February 6, 1995, and within the month had discovered the identity of the intruder...Kevin Mitnick. To discover precisely where Kevin was, however, Shimomura had to walk the streets of Raleigh, North Carolina with a device used to monitor cell telephone communications. A brief time later, the FBI, together with Shimomura in tow, obtained entrance to Mitnick's apartment and arrested him. It is interesting to notice that at the time of the arrest, Mitnick congratulated Shimomura to his own achievement. Therefore, in February 1995, Kevin Mitnick was arrested by the FBI while he was sitting in his apartment that was located at Raleigh, North Carolina. He had been charged with various federal crimes which were focused on two-to-three year time period in which he had been hacking into computer systems along with committing wire fraud. Several illegal paraphernalia were discovered in their apartment, including numerous bogus IDs, over 100 mobile phone codes for cloned phones, and needless-to-say, the cloned cellular phones themselves. The FBI charged Kevin with the following:

• Eight counts of possession of unauthorized access devices.
• Damage to computer systems
• Fourteen counts of wire fraud
• Unauthorized access to federal computer systems
• Wire/electronic communications intercepts

Then in 1999 Los Angeles, when it was all over, before the United States District Court for the Central District of California, Kevin pled guilty to the following as part of a plea agreement:

• Two counts of computer fraud
• One count of illegal wire communication interception
• Four counts of wire fraud

The courtroom in LA sentenced Kevin Mitnick into a prison term of 46 months along with an additional 22 weeks for breach of the terms of the 1989 supervised release sentencing that was associated with computer fraud. The violation of his 1989 supervised release provisions came to light when Kevin confessed to hacking into different computer systems such as the PacBell voicemail system. Associating with his co-defendant, Lewis De Payne, was also a violation of the 1989 sentencing. Overall, Kevin ended up being in prison for a little over five years, using four and a half years being served before his trial and eight months in solitary confinement. Why was Kevin in solitary confinement?

Well, it appears that during that Period of Time, federal judges Were so paranoid of Mitnick's skills that the FBI convinced a federal judge that Kevin may initiate a nuclear war by whistling the right tones into a phone, which could place him in contact with a NORAD modem, and that he could do so straight from the prison phone system.

In that period in time, that ended in January, 2003, Kevin had been, in the outset, barred from making use of any communications technology except for a landline telephone. Mitnick obtained a lawyer and went to fight this decision and finally won a ruling in his favor, permitting him Internet access. As part of the plea deal which has been agreed to, Mitnick was likewise prohibited to profit from films or books that were centered on his illegal actions for a pre-determined interval. However, close to the conclusion of the fourth quarter of 2002, an FCC judge released a judgment that Kevin Mitnick had been appropriately rehabilitated so he would currently possess an amateur radio license issued by an agency of the national government. As of this writing of this book, Kevin Mitnick now directs the Mitnick Security Consulting LLC and is part owner of a security firm named KnowBe4, a provider of an integrated platform focused on safety awareness training and phishing testing. Kevin Mitnick and what he has termed his "Global Ghost Team" now maintain a 100% effective track record of entering the safety of all procedures they have been paid to hack by utilizing a mix of social technology and technical exploits. As chief "white hat" hacker and chief executive officer in Mitnick Security Consulting LLC, Kevin acts as an adviser to executives, administration, and their respective staff on the theory and practice of social technology, a topic on which he is the principal global jurisdiction. Additionally, Kevin helps your normal everyday consumers in the way they could protect their data and themselves from harm using language that is readily understood. Adding to Kevin's responsibilities, he also functions as the chief hacking officer in KnowBe4, a coaching company that creates Kevin Mitnick's Security Awareness Training. Kevin's perceptions on current events are also highly sought after, leading to a high number of press appearances annually. He is among the most sought-after cybersecurity speakers and has been a commentator, safety analyst, or interviewee on a great number of information stations globally, such as Good Morning America along with 60 Minutes. He's also been called before Congress (both the House and the Senate) to testify on cybersecurity matters of interest to the United States. You can purchase Kevin's publications on Amazon and in other book distribution facilities. His books Art of Intrusion: The Real Story behind the Exploits of Hackers, Intruders and Deceivers, along with Art of Deception: Controlling the Human Element of Security. These novels are deemed compulsory readings for professionals focused in cybersecurity.

The 414s

The 414s named themselves after the area code of their hometown in Milwaukee, Wisconsin. These computer hackers ranged in age from 16 to 22 years old. In the early 1980s, they compromised numerous high-profile computer systems, including computers at Los Alamos National Laboratory located in Los Alamos, New Mexico, Sloan-Kettering Cancer Center located in New York City, and Security Pacific Bank located in Los Angeles, California. They met each other when they had been members of a regional Boy Scout Explorer post and were identified and investigated by the FBI in 1983. Patrick later asserted that the sole motivation he had for his illegal actions was the sheer challenge of breaking into systems he wasn't supposed to be in, and subsequently remaining undetected on those approaches. The majority of the systems they hacked were using Digital Equipment Corporation's VAX/VMS operating system. All in all, the 414s were accused of hacking into around 60 pc systems. Most viewed them as just harmless pranksters, like the film War Games that had been released earlier in 1983. Nonetheless, the 414s were not entirely innocent because they were responsible for damages of $1,500 in Sloan-Kettering during their June 3, 1983 hack because of how they deleted certain billing records, supposedly to cover their own tracks. Experts began to realize that others with nefarious motives could afterwards replicate their methods and do far worse damage. The 414s had merely made use of low-cost home personal computers and quite simple hacking methods, such as using default and common passwords and exploiting unpatched security holes. Of course, these types of exploits are still with us today in 2021.

Wondra, who had been 22 years of age at that time, was the first member of the 414s to be seen by the FBI. Wondra was staying in his mom's house during that time. He advised the FBI that he was just curious and having some fun. The majority of the 414s members weren't prosecuted, and arrangements were made that the 414s would stop their illegal computer activities and pay appropriate compensation to those harmed by their prior attacks.

Gerald, the systems manager who really discovered the 414's pc hack at Sloan-Kettering, left a message for the hackers and initiated contact with the FBI, who then set wiretaps and finally traced the calls back to Milwaukee, Wisconsin.

The activities of the 414s from the early 1980s forced the world to stop and think about cybercrime. Neal Patrick testified before the U.S. House of Representatives on September 26, 1983 concerning the perils of computer hacking. Also because of those efforts, six bills associated with computer crime were introduced in the House in 1983. Approximately 1 year later, three of the 414s were charged under a federal provision pertaining to cell calls, which carried a maximum sentence of six months in prison plus a fine of $500. In the end, however, only two associates, Gerald Wondra and a co-defendant, were found guilty on two counts of making harassing phone calls.

Chen Chui claimed that we actually gained from the

activities of the 414s. "Without them, we would not be conscious at so early a date as to just how internet currently being placed in homes and businesses around the country could be compromised. Without the nefarious Legislation and pc safety at an earlier date, than we would have suffered some tragedy. We owe the 414s a debt of gratitude however, as they possibly saved us from many future malicious attacks which could have done much more damage than the 411s ever did. They showed us how vulnerable our computer systems were. This allowed us to start building our defenses."

Legion of Doom

During its glory days from approximately 1984 to 1991, LOD (Legion of Doom) was generally considered to be the most skillful hacking group worldwide. Even now, in 2021, the LOD is regarded as among the most prominent hacking teams at the history of computer technology. The LOD was founded by a hacker code named Lex Luthor due to an argument with his former team, the Knights of Shadow. The LOD was split into LOD and Masters of Deception for its team members who were more technically proficient at hacking as opposed to only phreaking (making illegal phone calls). The general philosophies of the LOD and the Masters of Deception differed, but it is challenging to unravel the activities of both groups because there existed a crossover between the groups. Unlike the Masters of Deception, there were differing beliefs regarding just what the LOD was.

The LOD published the Legion of Doom Technical Journals and donated to the bundle of computer hacking wisdom at the time. They looked at themselves as not causing any direct harm to the telephone systems and computer programs they seized. Still, many LOD participants were arrested and prosecuted for instigating suspected harm to various computer and telephone systems.

It had been in the summer of 1984 that an idea had been

conceived that would finally permanently change the surface of the computer underground. Throughout that summer, a huge interest in computer telecommunications surged forth and placed a very high number of excited neophytes on the national computer scene. This throng of people was all seeking to learn as much as possible about computer systems, plus they started to overwhelm the nation's computer bulletin board telephone lines. From out of the pandemonium came a necessity for well-educated trainers to assist in passing on their personal computer system knowledge to the next wave of computer enthusiasts.

In 1984, one of the most popular computer bulletin boards at that time was a computer program in New York christened Plover-NET that was handled by an individual who titled himself Quasi-Moto. This bulletin board was heavily trafficked and a significant long distance carrier began blocking all of the phone calls to its number.

One of the system directors of Plover-NET was a person called Lex Luthor. At that moment, there existed only a couple of hacking groups, such as Fargo 4A, Knights of Shadow, and the LOD. Lex was admitted into Knights of Shadow in early 1984, but afterwards advocating a few new members and then having them rejected, Lex made the decision to create a new invitation-only bulletin board whose purpose was to produce a new pc hacking team.

Starting in May 1984, Lex commenced contacting people whom he had seen on bulletin boards such as Plover-NET alongside the people that he personally believed needed the type of superior knowledge that the hacking group he imagined should possess. Countless telephone calls and Alliance Teleconferences later, the people who made up the first LOD were gathered.

In 1992, several members of LOD constructed and maintained LODCOM, Inc., which collected older hacker bulletin board messages to archive, which was later to be sold. Most of this material (perhaps all of it) was afterwards moved to TextFiles.com.

Marauder later formed LOD.COM as a consulting company, and a few ex-LOD members set up reports on that system.

In the late 1990s, a root DNS server had an illicit new Top-Level Domain Name of LOD for at least a year. In 1989, the Secret Service made some significant discoveries in hacking circles, which led to the arrest of three members of this LOD. Bell South's phone network had been maliciously hacked into in 1988, and it was believed that these three people from LOD had perpetrated the deed. This led to prison time for Franklin Darden, Adam Grant, and Robert Riggs.

The Morris Worm

The Morris Worm was one of the earliest computer network worms dispersed via the Internet on November 2, 1988. It had been the first to achieve substantial mainstream media consideration. In addition, the worm caused the first felony conviction in America under the 1986 Computer Fraud and Abuse Act. The Morris worm was designed by a graduate student at Cornell University, a fellow who went by the name of Robert Tappan Morris, and started by a computer located at the Massachusetts Institute of Technology (MIT) campus.

According to Robert, the Morris worm was not created to cause harm, but rather primarily to ascertain the scope of the Internet. The worm was pushed out from an MIT computer system because Morris was hoping to deceive researchers into believing that its creator was at that location, which Morris wasn't (Morris is now a tenured professor at MIT).

The Morris worm functioned by exploiting well-known vulnerabilities in UNIX finger, sendmail, and remote shell (rsh) as well as weak passwords. Note that due to security and performance enhancements in the current computer networks, the Morris worm would no longer be effective in today's world.

The Morris worm has occasionally been nicknamed the "Great Worm" due to the exceptionally disturbing outcome it had on the Web during the time of its release, taking into consideration the overall system downtime and impact relative to the perception of safety and reliability of the Internet. The nickname has been taken from the "Great Worms" of Tolkien's Middle Earth Trilogy: Scatha and Glaurung.

The U.S. Government estimated the entire cost of the damage to be in the neighborhood of $100,000 to $10,000,000. Cliff Stoll, an astronomer and writer of The Cuckoo's Egg: Tracking a Spy Through the Maze of Computer Espionage, who assisted in the struggle against the worm, said in 1989 that he had taken a poll of the net and discovered that 2,000 computer systems had become infected within a 15-hour period of time, and at that time, virus removal took around two days. It's been reported that in the neighborhood of 6,000 UNIX systems were infected by the Morris worm. However, Morris's colleague, Paul Graham, claims that he had been present when this particular statistic was bandied about and a lot of it was just guesswork.

Several segments of the Internet were segmented off for a couple of days as regional networks dropped off the NSFNet backbone and disconnected from each other so as to thwart recontamination while they were in the process of cleaning up their own personal computer networks. This Morris worm episode triggered several corresponding reactions which became the center of considerable attention and unease throughout the coming years.

After a couple of appeals, Robert Morris was sentenced to three years' probation, 400 hours of community service, and a monetary fine of $10,050. The case was later sent to court as an appeal, but his conviction was upheld because the Morris worm was considered a threat not just to several individuals but also to various government institutions, research entities, and colleges and universities.

I mentioned that there were several responses to the worm. One of them was CERT, with the purpose to react and assist with responses to discovered computer vulnerabilities, among other things. Computer security expert Eugene Spafford said that the program held no code which could damage a computer system on which it ran. The worst that the program itself could do would be to exploit known vulnerabilities that would then allow the program to replicate itself and proliferate among other computer systems. It was, of course, this proliferation among a large number of computer systems that finally caused the Internet to malfunction.

An investigation of the source code denotes that Morris did attempt to keep the spread of the worm under his control (which does reveal he knew that this was a possible problem); nonetheless, he was far more confident in his coding skills than he should have been. Errors in his program resulted in numerous "sudden" system crashes on the Web (SunOS operating systems) and to executing a number of times on a number of other systems, consuming system resources. The major target of this program was a version of UNIX called BSD. The mistake that altered the worm from a hypothetically innocuous academic application into what was in effect a denial of service (DoS) attack was in the mechanisms of how the worm was created to spread, which subsequently brought down the Internet.

Ch. 2 History of Hacking 1990s

Nahshon Even-Chaim

Nahshon Even-Chaim, a.k.a. Phoenix, was born in May of 1971. He has the grand honor of becoming the first computer hacker of importance to be condemned in the land of Australia. He was highly regarded by his colleagues in The Realm, a group of computer hackers located in Melbourne, Australia.

Nahshon concentrated his malicious hacks on defense and nuclear weapons research networks. Nahshon initiated his hacking exploits via modem and breached computer programs by directly dialing into the computer network or via a telephone through X.25 networks. He, of course, shifted to Internet connectivity when it became available to him. He established a reputation among his Realm comrades of having both significant computer hacking skills together with being rather arrogant.

In late 1988, the AFP (Australian Federal Police) discovered his true identity by making use of informants. In June 1988, Australia brought to bear new legislation focused on computer crime that the AFP put to use, and subsequently they obtained a warrant in January 1990 to electronically eavesdrop on

Nahshon's phone dialogues, including the information transmitted via his modem. The digital wiretap on his voice telephone calls, which was initiated on January 26, 1990, was kept in place for several weeks, while the electronic data wiretap began about two weeks later and was kept in place for around a month and a half. The wiretaps were being scrutinized by the AFP in its Telephone Intercept Branch in Canberra, Australia, approximately 250 miles from Nahshon's home. The data intercepts revealed to the AFP that Nahshon spent a considerable amount of time on his computer, working hastily to break into and meddle in the affairs of others' computer systems. This is akin to breaking into someone's home or business when you think they can't observe your activities and then go about pilfering the place.

This was the first historically documented time where a remote computer communications data intercept was used to obtain evidence that could stand up in a court of law relative to some computer crime prosecution. Captured telephone voice transcripts revealed Nahshon's snickering with a fellow hacker pertaining to the way he was "f**king with NASA" and added, "Yeah, they're gonna actually want me bad. This is fun!" In a different dialog with a hacker from America, Nahshon claimed, "The guys down at the local universities are screaming with rage because they couldn't get rid of us. The Americans are getting pretty damn pissed off with me because I'm doing so much and they can't do much about it. I'm getting to the stage now where I can get into almost any system online. I have virtually raped the Web beyond belief".

Nahshon pled guilty to 15 charges, all of which involved his hacking into computer systems belonging to other people at Commonwealth Scientific and Industrial Research Organization in Melbourne, Australia, where he unlawfully replicated Zardoz, an ongoing report which was used to privately broadcast UNIX operating system security flaws to those in the computer industry that had a need to know - mostly universities and NASA. At the same time, the AFP forcefully entered into the homes of Jones and

Woodcock, his Realm colleagues.

Nahshon had racked up 48 offences against him and was charged with all 48. Of these 48 charges, the majority carried a maximum 10-year sentence in prison. On October 6, 1993, Nahshon negotiated an agreement where he would enter a guilty plea if the total charges were lowered to 15, received a sentence amounting to 500 hours of community service, and no more than one year in jail. The one-year stint in jail ended up being suspended by the court.

After his hacking career came to an end, Nahshon worked in the information technology area for a time and then moved on to different interests such as creating music.

Masters of Deception

The Masters of Deception (MOD) were a team of hackers residing in New York. Their big push was the manipulation of the telephone company infrastructure. During the 1980s and early 90s, mainframes and minicomputers were being used by telephone companies to control and perform administrative activities on the phone network.

In the beginning, MOD held training seminars for their members on Loop-Around Test Lines. As confidence and membership grew, MOD moved on to the hacking of RBOC phone switches as well as the afore-mentioned mainframes and minicomputers that controlled the telephone network.

The members of MOD were Mark Abene "Phiber Optik", Paul Stira "Scorpion", Elias Ladopoulos "Acid Phreak", John Lee "Corrupt", and Julio Fernandez "Outlaw". There were other MOD members like Supernigger (also of DPAK), Wing, Nynex Phreak, Billy the Kid, Crazy Eddie, The Plague, ZOD, Seeker, Red Knight (who was also a member of Cult of the Dead Cow), Lord Micro, n00gie, and Peaboy (a.k.a. MCI Sprinter), but their true names are not known since they were unable to do hacking feats of any real significance.

Members of MOD for some reason had a need to display their skills to other hackers and even demean other known hackers of that period in time. MOD would boast about their hacking adventures, which usually is the very thing that brings down hackers. Their partnerships and boastings included tapping into phone systems, stealing confidential credit reports and putting them up for sale, and various other things which were used to deride other hackers.

MOD members enjoyed toying with other hacker groups. One of them - the Legion of Doom - became one of their favorites to taunt. Note that Legion of Doom took its name from a villainous group of comic book fame. The rivalry between MOD and Legion of Doom apparently brought to bear both ethnic and class overtones. Unlike the common hackers of the 1980s (well-to-do suburbanites) whose parents had the money to spend on expensive computer equipment of that period in time, MOD was a multilingual melting pot of blue-collar New Yorkers involving Hispanics, blacks, Italians, Greeks, and Lithuanian youths.

MOD exploited computer systems belonging to others using (for the most part) relatively inexpensive home computers. Due to this type of membership history, they did not follow the regime of the normal hacker groups since most hacking teams had a propensity to come and go within around a six-month time period as members left for college, found a girlfriend, or even in some way, shape, or form "got a real life." But this didn't occur with MOD. MOD persisted in bringing into the fold new members from their monthly team meetings within the atrium of the Citicorp Building in Manhattan. MOD also made good use of a computer bulletin board named KAOS, which brought in new members. Relative to prior hacking groups, MOD operated somewhat differently. While they voluntarily pooled information with one another, they took a controversial outlook on sharing information with other hackers who were outside their group. It was known among MOD members that knowledge was power, and access to

MOD's knowledgebase has to be earned in a fashion like the martial arts, via degrees (belts...white, green, purple, brown, black, etc.) of initiation and a demonstrated respect for their tradecraft, rather than simply releasing potent information into the wild where it could be utilized for immoral purposes. This informal compartmentalized protection of knowledge considered by MOD leadership to be more sensitive and valuable, similar to practices in the military and intelligence communities where information compartmentalization is actively and formally practiced on a daily basis, was a practice which was previously successfully utilized by the Legion of Doom during the 1980s. As stated by Lex Luthor, "I recognized early on that only certain people can be trusted with specific information, and particular types of information can be trusted to nobody. Giving out useful things to irresponsible people would necessarily lead to whatever thing it was being abused and no more useful. I was very possessive of my advice and frequently withheld things from my posts".

MOD had five of its group members brought up on charges and indicted in federal court in 1992 because of the efforts of a joint FBI/Secret Service task force. Geoffrey Berman and Stephen Fishbein were both assistant U.S. attorneys out of the U.S. Attorney's Office (Southern District of New York) who prosecuted the MOD case. On July 16, 1992, five members of MOD pled not guilty in court on all fees levied by the U.S. federal government. The serious charges levied against them involved hacking into very powerful computer systems, stealing a large number of credit reports of various individuals, and then selling those confidential reports to others, such as private investigators. This is like breaking into someone's house, finding where they keep their valuable financial information, and then photographing it with a camera to later sell to somebody willing to pay for the information. In many states within the United States, walking in and finding someone in your home stealing your financial information would lead to the trespassers and thieves being shot dead right there in the home.

Over the next six months (we have moved into 1993 now), all five members of MOD pled guilty due to the insurmountable evidence stacked against them and were subsequently sentenced to either probation or time in prison. After Mark Abene was sentenced, 2600: The Hacker Quarterly, winter 1993--1994, displayed a rag doll on its cover called "Berman" being pierced by a knife.

Operation Sun Devil

In 1990, Operation Sun Devil was launched by the United States Secret Service (USSS) and grew into a nationwide orchestrated crackdown on computer hacking teams situated throughout the USA. The name Sun Devil comes from the Arizona State University (ASU) Sun Devil football stadium, which is in close proximity to the local Secret Service headquarters from which the investigation and federal government raids were coordinated.

It involved forays into roughly 15 U.S. metropolitan regions and led to numerous arrests and the confiscation of computers, computer bulletin board networks, and various storage media. The arrests and ensuing court cases brought about the establishment of the Electronic Frontier Foundation.

Operation Sun Devil has also been viewed as one of the previous assaults on the Legion of Doom and other hacking groups. In the years prior to the 1990s, there existed people within the USA who enjoyed the manipulation of phone systems, known as phreakers, and it was rare for them to be prosecuted in any real way. The majority of phreakers used tones made by electromechanical boxes or software to obtain calling card numbers to be able to enable themselves and their buddies to make telephone calls at no cost. But a small group of technical phreakers were more interested in technology related information that pertained to the inner workings of the telecommunication system. Telephone companies began complaining to law enforcement about the financial losses they were incurring from illegal phreaking activities. The unfortunate side is that telephone execs must have taken into account the losses but chose not to devote the necessary monies to boost security for the new digital phone network and training for their workers, and rather tossed the burden they had of blocking the phreakers on the shoulders of law enforcement and the general public. The change from analog to digital equipment started to uncover much more of the internal workings of telephone company networks as malicious hackers started to deconstruct the internal networks, including switches and trunks. Due to absence of legislation and proficiency on the part of U.S. law enforcement, there were very few successful prosecutions against hackers until the Operation Sun Devil was launched.

None-the-less, starting in 1989, the USSS, under Title 18, paragraph 1029, started investigating by making use of some new powers granted by Congress to deal with access-device fraud as an extension of wire fraud investigations. An 18-month-long analysis showed the USSS that extensive credit card and calling card fraud was taking place on a regular basis over state lines.

Operation Sun Devil permitted multiple federal law enforcement agencies, chiefly the Secret Service and the FBI, to obtain invaluable proficiency in combating this new criminal action practice as well as growing their respective agencies' annual budgets. Congress established new laws which were fashioned to allow federal prosecutors to charge malicious people accused of hacking, phreaking, and wire and credit card fraud. Evidence garnered from Operation Sun Devil permitted law enforcement organizations to convince the United States Congress of the need for extra funds, training, and overall capability expansion. Most of the raids by law enforcement happened in Arizona, which is exactly where all of the press conferences were held. These swoops usually occurred in typical middle-class suburbs and targeted credit card thieves and telephone system hackers/phreakers. These law enforcement raids were generally completed by the local authorities, with the assistance of approximately 150 U.S. Secret Service agents, CIA, and FBI. Nearly 30 search warrants were issued and executed on May 7 and 8, 1990, resulting in several arrests. Police also appropriated approximately 42 pc systems and about 25 bulletin board computer networks, including some of the most notorious and elite hacking bulletin boards existing worldwide during that period of time, such as the infamous Cloud Nine.

Up until this point in time, there has never been a greater shutdown of electronic bulletin boards. Storage devices didn't escape the dragnet either, with over 20,000 floppy disks seized by law enforcement. These storage devices contained many different types of data, of course, including malicious software, credit card details from tens of thousands of stolen accounts, and an overabundance of illegal copyrighted material.

Other portions of the operation targeted the underground hacking magazine Phrack, which had earlier published the contents of a proprietary text file mined from BellSouth computer systems and containing information pertaining to the E911 emergency response system. Garry M. Jenkins, assistant director of the USSS, said during an interview that, "the Secret Service is sending a clear message to those computer hackers who have decided to violate the laws of this state in the mistaken belief that they can successfully avoid detection by hiding behind the relative anonymity of their computer terminals".

Operation Sun Devil did terminate malicious hacking activities of lots of the world's finest hackers for a period of time, which is a really good reason that it has been acclaimed as a tactical victory due to the shock and damage the operation caused to the hacking community compared to the much longer battles conducted against entities such as the Legion of Doom.

The Brotherhood of Warez

Beginning in the first quarter of 1997, CBC radio aired a

disturbing story pertaining to the Tamai household in Emeryville, Ontario. It felt like something from a bad dream: lights flickering off and on haphazardly, nonstop phone calls with nobody on the other end of the line once the phone was answered with gurgling and groaning sounds coming through the telephone lines during normal phone calls, along with voicemail passwords being changed by an unknown entity. A hacker named Sommy took credit for those shenanigans, even talking right to the Tamai family through the phone at random times. The incident christened "The Emeryville Horror," mystified law enforcement police who were also disconnected from the Tamai family when they tried to phone them.

The phone company, the electric power company, and two distinct security organizations, one from NBC and another from the Discovery Channel, were all baffled. Among the strangest and creepiest hacks has been Sommy's ability to overhear and record dialogues that took place in their house and add them to their phone voicemail recordings. It appeared to be really the nefarious actions of supernatural entities. It became so bad that the Tamai family finally put their home up for sale. All this made for really great radio and television and a scapegoat for its impending trepidations anticipating the entire world in a cyberspace environment. The story was everywhere nationwide and even globally to some extent. But upon further investigation, the truth finally came out. It was that Sommy was actually the Tamai family's teenage son. In April 1997 (too bad it wasn't right on April 1, which is April Fool's Day), their son Billy finally admitted to being the perpetrator of the pranks following several hours of interrogation with the police department that asked that he come to the police station for questioning with regard to the strange events. Due to his age and the fact that the incidents all happened within his own home, he wasn't charged. The report stated that he was just an ordinary teenager and that it was just a hoax that got out of hand.

This explains, of course, just how he managed to record conversations that were occurring in the Tamai home, flip breaker switches in the basement of the house, and pop up in the center of ongoing telephone conversations.

Launched by a hacking group known as U4EA, the Brotherhood of Warez was a team of hackers from Canada and similar to many teams of hackers in the time period of telephone phreaking. It was obviously a reprisal against the Sommy story that was now being broadcast nationwide. A note of interest is that while the Brotherhood of Warez did have access to all of the CBC computer programs, they made no effort to take anything from these systems. They were just trying to send out their message and have it clearly understood. The CBC eventually had to improve the safety of its computer network.

Ch. 3 History of Hacking 2000s

Mafiaboy

Mafiaboy (real name Michael Calce) was a teenager living in West Island, Quebec. He was responsible for initiating numerous highly publicized denial-of-service (DoS) attacks in February 2000.

Mafiaboy also initiated a number of failed strikes against 9 of the 13 rootname pc systems. Per the Yankee Group, the estimated losses from the malicious attacks amounted to $1.2 billion, and the attack on Amazon cost between $200,000 and $300,000 each hour because of lost business trades. Loss of customer goodwill, corporate standing, and public confidence might have been even larger in the time, but in 2021, the adverse consequences caused by Mafiaboy imply nothing and haven't adversely affected online business for these corporations in the long term.

Throughout February 2000, Calce broke into Yahoo! with a project he coined Rivolta. Rivolta was a DoS attack in which computer systems became bombarded with various types of communications to the point where they can't perform their appropriate business functions correctly. During that period of time, Yahoo! was a multibillion-dollar online corporation and the number one leading search engine internationally.

Mafiaboy's Rivolta was able to disable the Yahoo! site for almost one hour. According to Calce, his overall goal in this endeavor was to establish supremacy for both himself and his group of hackers, TNT. Buy.com was closed down in reaction to Calce's attacks. Calce reacted to this by shutting down Amazon, eBay, CNN, and Dell.com through a dispersed denial-of-service (DDoS) attack during the subsequent week.

Moving along to the end of this story, while testifying at a congressional hearing in the area of Washington, DC, computer security expert Winn Schwartau said that "Government and industrial computer programs are so badly protected now they can basically be considered defenseless--an Electronic Pearl Harbor waiting to happen". Whether we're referring to banking, social networking, or internet searches and several other kinds of web accounts, a significant number of individuals have an assortment of private information online.

Mafiaboy was the first to show just how available this information is to the public at large and how simple it is for nefarious hackers to acquire and use it for illegal purposes. The simple fact that the world's biggest website could be jeopardized by a teenager became a widespread global concern because the Web was now considered by many as an essential part of the North American market. Due to such DDoS attacks on important business components, confidence in online shopping diminished among clients, and the American marketplace underwent a slight setback as a consequence.

On a more positive note however, former CIA agent Craig Guent gives credit to Mafiaboy for waking up the online business world and the American government to the serious safety problems prevalent at that time, which caused a considerable increase in online safety during the next 10+ years.

Operation Shady RAT – 2006

A deluge of all cyber-attacks started in mid-2006 as recounted by Dmitri Alperovitch, vice president of Threat Research at McAfee in August 2011. The series of assaults affected over 70 organizations, including multiple defense contractors, commercial businesses internationally, the United Nations, and the International Olympic Committee (IOC).

Operation Shady RAT (OSR) became a focused effort to get a period of time to compromise computer programs in targeted institutions with the intent of pilfering software source code, government keys, email archives, file storage systems, and also any form of valuable intellectual property. Operation Shady RAT, a name coined by Alperovitch as a take on the personal computer security industry acronym for Remote Access Tool, is clarified by McAfee as "a five-year operation that was targeted against one specific person." With the objective of increasing the degree of public consciousness in that time, McAfee published the most comprehensive evaluation ever shown of victim profiles from a five-year concentrated operation by one explicit celebrity. This is not a new type of attack, and also the vast majority of the victims had been able to recover from the attacks. It isn't clear though whether or not the majority comprehended the importance of the incursions or just wiped and reimaged the compromised computer programs without additional analysis into the information loss.

McAfee had detected all of the malware variants and other relevant indicators for many years using Generic Downloader.x and Common BackDoor.t heuristic signatures (individuals who've had previous experience with this particular antagonist could identify it from the usage of encrypted HTML comments in web pages which function as a control station to the infected computer system). On occasion, organizations' computer systems were compromised for over two decades prior to the attackers being discovered and eradicated. The identity of the attackers is unknown; nonetheless, based on a number of the methods utilized and the goals that were chosen, various security experts entertain the belief that the Chinese authorities accounts for the computer hacks.

The development of Shady Rat's activities offers further circumstantial evidence of Chinese participation in the strikes. The operation targeted a wide-ranging area of both people - and private-sector institutions in just about every nation in Southeast Asia - although none in the country of China.

In 2006, or possibly before, the incursions commenced by targeting eight associations, such as South Korean steel and construction companies, a South Korean government bureau, a U.S. Department of Energy laboratory, a U.S. real-estate firm, international-trade institutions of Asian and Western countries, and the ASEAN Secretariat. McAfee got access to a particular control and command (C&C) server utilized by the attackers and also accumulated system logs which introduced the complete size of the victim population since around mid-2006 when the system log group started.

Keep in mind though that the real attacks might have started much earlier, but that is the oldest proof McAfee has at this time for the start of these compromises. The compromises themselves were regular procedure for such targeted incursions: a spear-phishing e-mail containing an exploit is directed to an individual with the correct level of corporate access, and the link, when opened in an unpatched computer system, will elicit a downloading of this malware. The stated malware will subsequently execute and initiate a backdoor communication station to the C&C web server and interpret the instructions encoded in the hidden comments embedded in the page code. This is going to be quickly followed by hackers logging into the infected computer system and proceeding to quickly escalate privileges and move laterally within the organization's computer network to institute fresh persistent footholds via additional compromised computer programs running malware, as well as targeting for quick exfiltration the key data they came for in the first place.

After meticulous evaluation of the system logs, McAfee was amazed by the vast assortment of victim organizations and the boldness of the offenders. Although McAfee refrained from identifying the majority of the victims, McAfee believed that naming names was acceptable in certain circumstances, not with the goal of drawing attention to a particular victim, but to emphasize the fact that virtually every company is falling prey to these attacks, irrespective of whether they're the United Nations, a Fortune 100 company, a small, nonprofit think tank, even a national Olympic team, or even an unfortunate computer security firm.

The interest from the information held in the Western and Asian national Olympic Committees, in addition to the IOC and the World Anti-Doping Agency from the lead-up and abrupt follow-up to the 2008 Olympics, was quite interesting and theoretically pointed a finger at a state actor behind the incursions, since there seemed to be no commercial value to be obtained from those attacks. The presence of political nonprofits, like a personal Western organization focused on the global progress of a U.S. national security think tank, is again rather instructive.

Another interesting aspect that the logs revealed to McAfee is the tasking orders of the offenders as the decades have gone by. In 2006, the year that the logs began, McAfee saw just eight intrusions which included more than one on a South Korean steel and construction company, one on a Department of Energy Research Laboratory, U.S. real estate companies, global trade organizations of Asian and Western countries, and even one on the ASEAN Secretariat. (That last intrusion began in October, a month before the organization's yearly summit in Singapore, which also continued for another 10 months.)

In 2007, the number of attacks almost tripled to include a total of 29 companies and other organizations. That year, McAfee started to see new compromises of no fewer than four U.S. defense contractors, Vietnam's government-owned technology firm, U.S. federal government agency, several U.S. state and county authorities, and one computer system Safety Company. The compromises of the Olympic Committees of two nations in Asia and a single Western country began that year as well. These measures led to the perpetrators to correct their code and employ a new type of attack which covered a lot of their tracks (causing their actions to vanish from the logs so that they couldn't be examined).

Even news media wasn't immune to the targeting, with at least one major U.S. news organization compromised at its New York headquarters and a Hong Kong agency which was infiltrated for over 21 months. The shortest time an organization stayed compromised was significantly less than one month; nine have that honor: IOC, Vietnam's government-owned technology firm, a trade association of a nation in Asia, one Canadian government agency, one U.S. defense contractor, a U.S. general government builder, a U.S. state and one county government, plus a U.S. bookkeeping firm.

McAfee must, however, warn that this may not necessarily be a sign of the rapid response of data security teams in these organizations, but maybe merely evidence that the perpetrator was interested only in a fast smash-and-grab operation which did not require a persistent compromise of the victims.

The maximum compromise was recorded at an Olympic Committee of a nation in Asia; it lasted off and on for 28 months, finally terminating in January 2010. What sets OSR aside from typical virus infections or intrusions is that the hackers involved seem to have been thinking of the long duration: accessing the computers that they compromised over periods of weeks or years rather than carrying out smash-and-grab raids to steal as far as they can as soon as possible for immediate monetary gain.

The bottom line is that associations are targets for one reason or another and that they must take suitable precautions to safeguard themselves and their staff. Precautions cut across physical, human, and technical steps. These measures should be implemented through comprehensive policies and procedures that are conveyed to employees and other stakeholders beginning with their debut and orientation into the business and that only end once the connection with the company stops. Periodic, realistic, and engaging training has to be ongoing to make certain that the policies and procedures are being followed and employees are aware and engaged, and to validate that the protective steps match the current threat.

Zeus – 2007

Zeus, ZeuS, or Zbot is a Trojan horse malware bundle that runs on versions of Microsoft Windows. Even though it can be used to execute many malicious and criminal tasks, it's often utilized to steal banking information from man-in-the-middle browser attacks, keystroke logging, and form catching. It is also utilized to set up the CryptoLocker ransomware.

Zeus is spread mainly through drive-by downloads and phishing schemes. First identified in July 2007 as it was used to steal information from the United States Department of Transportation, it turned into more widespread in March 2009.

In October 2010, the FBI announced that hackers from Eastern Europe had managed to infect computers around the globe using Zeus. The virus has been distributed in an e-mail, and if targeted individuals at businesses and municipalities opened the e-mail, the Trojan applications installed itself on the victimized computer, secretly capturing passwords, account numbers, and other data used to log in to online banking accounts. The hackers then used this information to take over the victims' bank accounts and also to make unauthorized transfers of tens of thousands of dollars at a time, often routing the money to other accounts controlled by a network of cash mules, which were paid a commission.

Many of the U.S. currency mules were recruited from overseas. They created bank accounts using fake documents and bogus names. Once the money was in the account, the mules would wire it back to their own bosses in Eastern Europe or draw it out in cash and smuggle it out of the country. Over a hundred people were arrested on charges of conspiracy to commit bank fraud and money laundering, over 90 from the United States, along with others in the UK and Ukraine. Members of this ring had stolen $70 million.

In 2013, Hamza Bendelladj, called Bx1 online, was arrested in Thailand and deported to Atlanta, Georgia. Early reports stated that he had been the mastermind behind ZeuS. He had been accused of working SpyEye (a bot functionally similar to ZeuS) botnets and suspected of operating ZeuS botnets. He had been charged with various counts of wire fraud and computer fraud and abuse. Court papers claimed that from around 2009 to 2011, Bendelladj and a list of others not only developed, but also marketed and sold various versions of the SpyEye virus and its various component parts online and allowed cybercriminals to personalize their purchases to include tailor-made procedures of obtaining victims' personal and financial data.

It was also alleged that Bendelladj advertised SpyEye on Internet forums devoted to cyber and other crimes, and managed command and control (C&C) servers. The charges in Georgia relate only to SpyEye, as there was a SpyEye botnet management server which had been established in Atlanta.

The Zeus threat is really composed of 3 components: a toolkit, the actual Trojan virus, and the C&C server. The toolkit is used to create the threat, the Trojan modifies the compromised computer, and the C&C server is used to monitor and manage the Trojan.

Trojan.Zbot is created using a toolkit that's readily available on underground marketplaces used by online offenders. There are various versions available, from free ones (frequently backdoored themselves) to all those an attacker must pay up to US$1000 in order to use. These marketplaces also offer additional Zeus-related providers, from bulletproof hosting for C&C servers to rental of already-established botnets. Regardless of the model, the toolkit can be used for two things. The attacker may edit and then compile the setup file into a .bin file. Second, they could compile an executable, which is then sent to the potential victim through various means. This executable is what's normally called the Zeus Trojan or even Trojan.Zbot.

The huge danger was that for the first time, almost anyone could use this toolkit user interface because it was made so simple and fast. Many would-be criminals were now able to find a piece of the action. Coupling this with the multitude of illicit copies of the toolkit circulating on the black market makes sure that Trojan.Zbot continues to be one of the most popular and widely seen Trojans on the threat landscape. While unusual in the current threat landscape, Trojan.Zbot tends to utilize lots of the exact same file names across variations. Given the way in which the toolkit works, every revision tends to stick to the exact same file names once the executables are made.

While the first executable can be called whatever the attacker needs it to be, the files mentioned in the following subsections refer to the names used by the currently known toolkits. The location that Trojan.Zbot attaches itself to depends on the level of privileges the logged-in user account has at the time of infection. If the user is an administrator, the files are placed in the %System% folder. If not, they are copied to %UserProfile%\ Application Data. Trojan.Zbot generally creates a copy of itself using one of the following file names:

• ntos.exe
• oembios.exe
• twext.exe
• sdra64.exe
• pdfupd.exe

The threat creates a folder named "lowsec" in either the %System% or %UserProfile%\Application Data folder and then drops one of the following files into it:

• video.dll
• sysproc32.sys
• user.ds
• ldx.exe

While the extensions change here, these are all text-file variations of this setup file previously created and then compiled into the Trojan with the Zeus toolkit. This document includes any web pages to monitor, in addition to a list of websites to block, such as those that belong to security businesses. It can also be updated by the attacker with the danger of backdoor capabilities. Here is a portion of a sample configuration file:

Entry "DynamicConfig"
url_loader "http://[REMOVED].com/zeusbot/
ZuesBotTrojan.exe"
url_server "http://[REMOVED].com/zeusbot/gate.php"
file_webinjects "webinjects.txt"
Entry "AdvanccdConfigs"
;
end
entry "WebFilters"
"!http://[REMOVED].com"
"https:// [REMOVED].com/*"
"!http://[REMOVED].ru/*"
end
entry "WebDataFilters"
; "! http://[REMOVED].ru/*" "passw;login"
end
entry "WebFakes"
; "http://[REMOVED].com" "http://[REMOVED].com" "GP"
"" ""
end

entry "TANGrabber"
"https://[REMOVED].com/*/jba/mp#/SubmitRecap.do"
"S3C6R2" "SYNC_TOKEN=*" "*"
end
entry "DnsMap"
;127.0.0.1
end
end

A second file is dropped into the "lowsec" folder, with one of the following file names:

• audio.dll
• sysproc86.sys
• local.ds

This file serves as a storage text file for any stolen information. When a password is obtained by the threat, it is saved in this file and later sent to the attacker. In addition, the threat adds itself to the registry to start when Windows starts, using one of two sub keys:

• HKEY_ LOCAL _MACHINE \ SOF TWAR E \ Microsoft\WindowsNT\CurrentVersion\Winlogon\"Userinit" = "%System%\userinit.exe, %System%\sdra64.exe"
• HKEY_CURRENT_USER\SOFTWARE\Microsoft\ Windows\CurrentVersion\Run\"userinit"+"%UserProfile%\ Application Data\sdra64.exe"

If the logged-in account at the time of infection has administrative privileges, the very first entry is created. If the account has restricted privileges, the next is utilized.

Depending on the level of privileges, Trojan.Zbot will inject itself in one of two ways. If it's not successful, it tries to do exactly the same thing using the explorer.exe support. The threat also injects code to some svchost.exe providers, which it later uses when stealing banking information. Once installed, Trojan.Zbot will automatically gather a lot of information about the compromised computer, and then it sends that information back to

the C&C server. This information includes the following:
• A unique bot identification string
• Name of the botnet
• Version of the bot
• Operating system version
• Operating system language
• Local time of the compromised computer
• Uptime of the bot
• Last report time
• Country of the compromised computer
• IP address of the compromised computer
• Process names

The core purpose of Trojan.Zbot would be to steal passwords and that is evident by the different methods it goes about doing so. Upon setup, Trojan.Zbot will immediately check Protected Storage (PStore) for passwords. It specifically targets passwords used in Internet Explorer, along with access to FTP and POP3 accounts. Also, in Internet Explorer, all of the cookies are deleted. In this way the user needs to log in again to any commonly visited websites, and also the threat could list the log-in credentials at that moment.

A more flexible method of password-stealing utilized by the threat is driven by the configuration file during web browsing. After the attacker creates the configuration file, they are able to include any URLs they wish to monitor. When any of those URLs are visited, the danger accumulates as any usernames and passwords typed within these pages is stolen. In order to accomplish that, it hooks the functions of various DLLs, taking charge of network functionality. The following is a list of DLLs and the APIs within them that are used by Trojan.Zbot:

WININET.DLL
• HttpSendRequestW
• HttpSendRequestA
• HttpSendRequestExW

- HttpSendRequestExA
- InternetReadFile
- InternetReadFileExW
- InternetReadFileExA
- InternetQueryDataAvailable
- InternetCloseHandle

WS2_32.DLL and WSOCK32.DLL
- send
- sendto
- closesocket
- WSASend
- WSASendTo

USER32.DLL
- GetMessageW
- GetMessageA
- PeekMessageW
- PeekMessageA
- GetClipboardData

Trojan.Zbot can also inject other fields into the web pages it monitors. In order to accomplish this, it intercepts any page being returned to the computer which is compromised and adds some extra fields. For example, if a user requests a page from his or her bank's website, and the bank returns a page requiring a username and password, the threat can also be configured to inject a third field asking for the user's Social Security Number.

This threat is known to infect computers through a number of methods:

- Spam e-mails: threat using spam campaigns. The subject material varies from 1 campaign to the next, but often focuses on current events or attempts to trick the user with e-mails purported to come from well-known institutions like FDIC, IRS, Twitter, Facebook, or Microsoft. The attackers behind Trojan.Zbot have made a concerted effort to spread their virus to as many places as possible.

- Drive-by downloads: The authors behind Trojan.Zbot also have been seen using exploit packs to disperse the danger via drive-by download strikes. When an unsuspecting user visits one of these websites, a vulnerable computer will get infected with the threat. The particular ways used to spread the threat change, largely based on the proliferation and ease-of-use of exploits available in the world at the time the Trojan is distributed.

So far, Trojan.Zbot has been seen using the following vulnerabilities:

- AOL Radio AmpX ActiveX Control 'ConvertFile()' Buffer Overflow Vulnerability (BID 35028)
- Microsoft Active Template Library Header Data Remote Code Execution Vulnerability (BID 35558)
- Microsoft Internet Explorer ADODB.Stream Object File Installation Weakness (BID 10514)
- Snapshot Viewer for Microsoft Access ActiveX Control Arbitrary File Download Vulnerability (BID 30114)
- Adobe Reader 'util.printf()' JavaScript Function Stack Buffer Overflow Vulnerability (BID 30035)
- Adobe Acrobat and Reader Collab 'getIcon()' JavaScript Method Remote Code Execution Vulnerability (BID 34169)
- Adobe Reader and Acrobat (CVE-2009-2994) U3D 'CLODMeshDeclaration' Buffer Overflow Vulnerability (BID 36689)
- Adobe Acrobat and Reader Multiple Arbitrary Code Execution and Security Vulnerabilities (BID 27641)

Symantec has recommended everybody, including administrators, follow their security best practices listed here:

- Use a firewall to block all incoming connections from the web going to services that shouldn't be publicly available. By default, you need to deny all incoming links and only enable services you explicitly need to supply to the outside world. Enforce a password policy. Complex passwords make it difficult to crack password files on computers. This helps to prevent or limit damage when a computer is infected.

- Make sure that programs and users of the computer use the bottom level of privileges required to finish a task. When prompted for an admin password, then make sure that the program asking for administration-level accessibility is a valid program.

- Disable the AutoPlay function to prevent the automatic launching of executable files. Disconnect drives when not required. When write access is not required, enable read-only mode.

- Turn off file when not needed. If file sharing is required, use ACLs so that access is limited. Eliminate anonymous access to shared folders. Only allow user accounts with strong passwords have access to shared folders.

- Turn off all unnecessary services. By default, operating systems often run services that are not critical. These services are paths of attack. If they are removed, threats have less paths of attack.

- If a threat exploits one or more network services, block access to those services until a patch is applied.

- Always keep your patch levels up-to-date, especially on computers that host public services such as HTTP, FTP, mail, and DNS.

- Have your e-mail server block or remove e-mail that contains attachments that are commonly used to spread threats, such as .vbs, .bat, .exe, .pif, and .scr files.

- Isolate infected computers quickly to prevent threats from spreading further.
- Train employees that it not a good idea to open attachments if they aren't expecting them. Just visiting a malicious website can cause an infection if the browser's security is weak.
- If Bluetooth is not needed on mobile devices, turned it off. If you need to use it, make sure that the device's visibility is set to "Hidden" so that it can't be scanned by other Bluetooth devices. Never accept applications that are not signed or if they were sent by an unkown device.

Ch. 4 History of Hacking 2010s

Stuxnet – 2010

Although neither state has supported this publicly, anonymous U.S. officials speaking to the Washington Post claimed the worm was designed during the Obama administration to sabotage Iran's nuclear program with what might seem to be a lengthy series of unfortunate accidents.

Exploiting four zero-day flaws, (a zero-day flaw is one that has not yet been documented and protected against) Stuxnet works by targeting machines using the Microsoft Windows operating system and programs, then seeking out Siemens Step7 software. Stuxnet reportedly compromised Iranian PLCs (programmable logic controllers – computers used for controlling industrial machines), amassing information on industrial systems and also causing the fast-spinning centrifuges to rip themselves apart.

Stuxnet's architecture isn't domain-specific which means that it could be tailored as a platform for attacking modern Supervisory Control and Data Acquisition (SCADA) and PLC systems, most of which reside in Europe, Japan, and the United States. Stuxnet allegedly ruined nearly one-fifth of Iran's nuclear centrifuges.

Ralph Langner, the researcher who discovered that Stuxnet infected PLCs, first speculated openly in September 2010 that the malware was of Israeli source, which it targeted Iranian nuclear facilities. However, Langner more recently, in a TED Chat recorded in February 2011, said that, "My opinion is that the Mossad is involved, but that the leading force is not Israel. The leading force behind Stuxnet is the cyber superpower--there's just one; and that's the United States." Langner called the malware "a one-shot weapon" and said that the planned target was probably struck, although he confessed that this was speculation.

Another spokesman named Frank Rieger, a writer who was also a member of the Chaos Computer Club, was the first to speculate that Natanz was the goal. The worm was at first identified by the security company VirusBlokAda in mid-June 2010. Journalist Brian Krebs's blog posting on July 15, 2010 was the first widely read report on the worm.

The group VirusBlokAda gave the worm the name "Rootkit.Tmphider", but Symantec called it "W32.Temphid". They later changed it to "W32.Stuxnet". Its current name comes from a blend of several key words from the program (".stub" and "mrxnet.sys").

Experts believe that Stuxnet took the biggest and costliest development effort in the malware background. Developing its many capabilities would have required a group of highly competent developers, in-depth knowledge of industrial processes, and an interest in attacking industrial infrastructure.

Eric Byres, who has years of experience maintaining and troubleshooting Siemens systems, informed Wired that composing the code would have taken many man-months, if not years. Symantec estimates that the team creating Stuxnet would have consisted of anywhere from 5 to 30 people and might have taken six months to prepare. Even the Guardian, the BBC, and The New York Times all claimed that (unnamed) experts analyzing Stuxnet consider that the complexity of the code suggests that only a state actor would possess the abilities to create it.

The source is unknown beyond rumor, however. The self-destruct along with other defenses within the code could imply that a Western government was accountable, or at least is responsible for the development of it.

Software security expert Bruce Schneier originally hailed the 2010 news coverage of Stuxnet as despicable, however, stating that it had been almost entirely based on speculation. But after subsequent research, Schneier said in 2012 that "we can now link Stuxnet into the centrifuge structure in the Natanz nuclear enrichment lab in Iran".

Stuxnet contains three modules: a worm that executes all routines related to the main payload of this attack; a link file that automatically implements the propagated copies of the worm; and a rootkit component accountable for hiding all malicious files and processes, preventing detection of the presence of Stuxnet. Stuxnet is generally released into the target environment via an infected USB flash drive. The worm then spreads across the system, scanning for Siemens Step7 software on computers controlling a PLC. In the absence of either criterion, Stuxnet becomes inactive inside the computer. If the conditions are fulfilled, Stuxnet introduces the infected rootkit on the PLC and Step7 applications, changing the codes and providing unexpected controls into the PLC while returning a loop of regular operations system values feedback to the users.

Stuxnet requires specific slave variable-frequency drives (frequency converter drives) to be attached to its targeted Siemens S7-300 system and its related modules. It only strikes those PLC systems with variable-frequency drives from two particular vendors: Vacon established in Finland and Fararo Paya based in Iran. Not only that but also monitors the frequency of the attached motors and only attacks systems which spin between 807 and 1,210 Hz. The industrial uses of motors with these parameters are varied and might include pumps or gas centrifuges.

Stuxnet installs malware to memory block DB890 of the PLC that tracks the Profibus messaging bus of the machine. When certain criteria are satisfied, it occasionally modifies the frequency to 1,410 Hz then to 1,064 Hz, and thus affects the performance of the connected motors by changing their rotational speed. It also installs a rootkit--the first such documented case with this platform--which hides the malware on the machine and then masks the changes in rotational rate from monitoring systems.

In 2015, Kaspersky Labs' research findings on another exceptionally sophisticated espionage platform created by what they referred to the Equation Group noted that the group had used two of the identical zero-day attacks utilized by Stuxnet, before they had been used in Stuxnet, and their usage in both programs was comparable. The people researching it said that both exploits had a similar type of usage that collectively was in various different computer worms, at around the same time, signals that the EQUATION group along with also the Stuxnet programmers are either the same or working closely together.

Kaspersky Labs experts initially estimated that Stuxnet started spreading around March or even April 2010, but the very first variant of the worm appeared in June 2009.

On July 15, 2010, the day the worm's presence became widely known, a distributed denial-of-service attack was made on the servers for just two leading mailing lists on industrial systems security. This attack, from an unknown source but likely associated with Stuxnet, disabled one of the lists and thereby disrupted an important source of information regarding power plants.

The next version, with substantial improvements, emerged in March 2010, seemingly because its authors thought that Stuxnet wasn't spreading fast enough; a third, with slight improvements, appeared in April 2010. The worm contained a component with a build time stamp from February 3, 2010. In the UK on November 25, 2010, Sky News reported it had obtained advice from an anonymous source for an unidentified IT security organization which Stuxnet, or a variation of this worm, had been traded on the black market. Siemens has launched a detection and removal tool for Stuxnet. Siemens recommended people call their customer support if an infection was detected. They also advised installing Microsoft security updates and prohibiting the use of third-party flash drives. Siemens also advised immediately upgrading password codes. The worm's ability to reprogram outside PLCs may complicate the removal procedure.

Symantec's Liam O'Murchu warned that mending Windows systems might not completely fix the infection; a comprehensive audit of PLCs may be necessary. Despite speculation that incorrect removal of this worm could lead to damage, Siemens reports that in the first four months since discovery, the malware has been successfully removed from the systems of 22 customers without any adverse impact.

The reason behind the discovery of Stuxnet is attributed to the virus accidentally spreading beyond its intended target (the Natanz plant) because of a programming error introduced in an update. This led into the centrifuges and spread further whenever an engineer returned home and connected his computer to the net.

The most valuable things we learned from the Stuxnet attack was the following:

- Stuxnet spread between sites through thumb drives. Poor USB device control allowed it to happen. Some people ended up gluing USB ports shut. A lot of people changed procedures to send all of their information through firewalls.
- Stuxnet spread through networks for many months before being detected. Some people pressured the vendors for faster security updates, and possibly invested a bit more in patch management.
- Stuxnet spread through IT/OT firewalls on SQL Server connections using a Siemens S7 hard-coded

password. Hard-coded passwords are a serious best-practice violation. Active Directory servers should be used to centralize all password policies and password management.

- Control networks can be different sometimes: Industrial sites are particularly vulnerable, and just a little bit of sabotage can cause lasting damage. Stuxnet is responsible for destroying thousands of uranium centrifuges.

- Any site can be hacked: The first law of cybersecurity is that no site is ever completely secure. Given enough time, money, and talent, any site can be hacked—even a uranium enrichment site with mil-spec protections. Every vulnerability assessment must at least have some way in which the site can be hacked. It is also a good idea to use terminology that the executives will understand.

- Training is essential to defense: In Stuxnet's case, the target was militarily strategic; the attackers were nation-state militaries prepared to spend billions on the attack if necessary, because it's still far cheaper than a conventional conflict. Attacks using trust relationships has become commonplace.

Shell shock – 2014

Shellshock, or Bashdoor, is a group of security bugs found in the widely used Unix Bash shell, the earliest of which was disclosed on September 24, 2014. Many Internet-facing providers, like some internet server deployments, use Bash to process certain requests, allowing an attacker to create exposed versions of Bash to perform arbitrary commands. This will enable an attacker to gain unauthorized access to a computer system.

Bash is present on many Linux, BSD, and Unix systems, such as Mac OS X. On September 12, 2014, Stéphane Chazelas called Bash's chief, Chet Ramey, telling Ramey about his discovery of the original bug, which he called "Bashdoor". Working with safety experts, he soon had a patch as well. The bug was assigned the CVE identifier CVE-2014-6271. It was announced to the general public on September 24, 2014, when Bash updates together with the fix were prepared for distribution. The initial bug causes Bash to unintentionally execute commands when the controls are concatenated to the end of function definitions stored at the values of environmental variables.

Attackers used Shellshock within only a few hours of its first disclosure simply by creating botnets of infected computers to execute distributed denial-of-service (DoS) attacks and vulnerability scanning. Security companies recorded countless attacks and probes related to the bug in the days following the disclosure. Shellshock could undermine millions of unpatched servers and other systems. Because of this, many have compared it to the Heartbleed bug due to its destructiveness.

Apple Inc. commented that OS X systems are safe from default, unless users configure innovative UNIX services. Such innovative users are usually capable of turning the services off until an official OS X patch is available, or they might use X code to substitute system-provided Bash using a custom-compiled variant that integrates unofficial patches.

Even though the company was notified of the danger before it was made public, they didn't release an upgrade until September of 2014. On September 24, 2014, details of this Shellshock bash bug arose. This bug caused people to scramble in an effort to quickly patch computers, routers, servers, firewalls, and other device which had vulnerable versions of bash.

The Shellshock problem is an example of a random code execution (ACE) vulnerability. Typically, ACE vulnerability strikes are implemented on programs which are running and need a highly sophisticated understanding of the internals of code implementation, memory layout, and assembly language--in short, this type of attack requires an expert.

Attackers can also use the ACE vulnerability as a way to upload a program which can be used to control a targeted device. Usually this is done by running what is known as a "shell". Shellshock is a significant problem since it removes the need for technical knowledge and gives an easy way of taking control of another computer (like a web server) and which makes it run code.

Suppose for a moment that you wished to strike a web server and make its CD or DVD drive slide available. There is actually a command on Linux that will do this: bin/eject. When a web server is exposed to Shellshock you could attack it by incorporating the magical series ():; to bin/eject then sending that series to the target pc over HTTP. Usually, the User-Agent string identifies the type of browser that you're using. Although in the case of this particular Shellshock vulnerability, it can be set to say anything.

In keeping an eye on the Shellshock attacks, Cloud Flare had actually been able to see someone attempting that very specific attack. So, if you run a web server and suddenly locate an abysmal DVD, it might be a sign your machine is vulnerable to Shellshock. Given that the bash environment is used in many configurations including CGI, ssh, rsh, rlogin, etc., those services may be impacted by this bug. Any internet servers which have user input and consume them in a party environment are also vulnerable. And this will create a new document new_file for your attacker.

Web applications are the largest exposure layer for this particular vulnerability. Keep in mind that this can manifest itself through several other services as noted above. The Common Vulnerability Scoring System foundation score for Shellshock is the highest potential - a 10 - that suggests its criticality.

For CIOs that are looking to know the extent of the problem, a fantastic documentation of the system and network is key. A vulnerability scan of these systems is also very significant. This should highlight Shellshock vulnerability. Keep in mind that a vulnerability scan that is done without logging into scanned systems can only reveal part of the picture. Because of this, it's strongly recommended to utilize the whole potential of this scanning tool and also do an authenticated scan. When it comes to fixing the Shellshock problem, the patch is very easy and well recorded. Yet, employing this in a large network may be a gigantic task. Large organizations should determine which systems are most vulnerable and focus on securing them first. By way of instance, a server in a demilitarized zone that has Apache but not computer-generated imagery being used can wait somewhat longer to get a patch, in comparison to a secure-shell server utilized as a management jump server for system admins and third parties.

Moreover, an attempted Shellshock attack can be very easily detected by means of a host or network intrusion detection system. Set it up to look for an attack and act appropriately.

HSBC Online Cyber Attack – 2016

HSBC clients were locked out of Internet banking for many hours on January 29, 2016, after the business was targeted by online criminals in a denial-of-service assault.

The lender, which has 17 million personal banking and business customers in the UK, said its site was attacked, but it had successfully defended its systems. Customers were not able to log into their accounts until late in the afternoon, on what's very likely to happen to be a hectic day for internet banking, as many workers received their first pay packet of the year. The bank said that there were not any signs of customer data theft.

This cyber-attack came less than a month after HSBC suffered a systems failure, which blocked customers from using its website and mobile app for almost two days.

Robert Capps of Tech Company NuData Security said that distributed denial-of-service (DDoS) attacks were designed to annoy and harass. He said that the idea of a DoS attack is to harass, intimidate, and embarrass a targeted institution, however the DDoS attacks rarely result in any lasting impact on any personal account at any institution. But he did say that the strikes had been used as a cover for different activities, such as cyber-heists, at a targeted institution. He said that sometimes it is meant to draw the attention of the information security teams of a particular bank from the real intent of the strikes, sometimes large money transfers, or even the theft and removal of customer account data.

People had to wait and see if the HSBC cyber-attack was merely a DDoS attack or was a cover for a far more damaging intrusion into their systems.

Andrew Tyrie, who was chairman of the Treasury committee at the time, said that he had recently asked regulators to take action to secure the banks. He said that the bank's cyber security systems just don't seem to be able to do the job. This means that bank clients are using a substandard company. He also said that these kind of incidents are regular, and that is completely unacceptable. "Until this is sorted out, the public will remain more vulnerable than necessary into the risks of IT banking failures, including flaws in paying invoices, an inability to receive their own money, and unauthorized access to their own accounts."

Alex Kwiatkowski, a senior strategist at software group Misys, said that the attack was "very concerning" and "shines a bright spotlight" upon HSBC's systems weaknesses. "The person or persons responsible for attacking HSBC have decided to turn their cyber guns on this specific bank for an unknown reason." He then stated some extremist groups have tried to bring down various websites to showcase their abilities. He also stated that he thought that cyberattacks are more sophisticated today and that banks should put an excess of resources into protection of their systems.

HSBC endured another high-profile systems collapse in August of 2015, which delayed 275,000 client payments--just before the weekend.

Panama Papers – 2016

The Panama Papers are comprised of nearly 12 million leaked documents that detail fiscal and attorney--customer information for more than 214,488 offshore entities. It is speculated that a Panamanian law firm and corporate support supplier of Mossack Fonseca had created the documents - some of which date back to the 1970s.

The leaked documents illustrate how wealthy individuals and public officials have the ability to maintain personal financial information privately. While overseas business entities are frequently not illegal, colleagues discovered that a number of those Mossack Fonseca shell corporations were used for prohibited purposes, including fraud, kleptocracy, tax evasion, and evading international sanctions.

"John Doe," the whistleblower who leaked the documents to German newspaper Süddeutsche Zeitung (SZ), stays anonymous, even to the journalists about the analysis. He told them that he thought that his life was at risk. In a May 6, 2016, announcement, John Doe cited earnings inequality as the reason for his actions, and said he leaked the records simply because he understood enough about what they contained to know the scale of the injustices they described. He also stated that he had never worked for any government agency. He showed that he would be willing to help prosecutors if they would make him immune to prosecution.

After SZ verified that the announcement did come from the Panama Papers source, ICIJ submitted the complete record on its website. The attacker's point of entry was an old variant of popular open source web server applications Drupal and WordPress. In the case of WordPress, a specific plugin was the probable culprit. "We think it's probable that an attacker gained access to the MF (Mossack Fonseca) WordPress website by means of a famous Revolution Slider vulnerability," based on Mark Maunder, Wordfence Founder and CEO, "this vulnerability is trivially easy to exploit." Simply download and run a very simple utility from a hacker site and the utility instantly provides attackers with shell access on the web server, which means they are now able to navigate the server's file system at will, uploading, downloading, and implementing documents however they enjoy.

Usually, any company that hosts its own web server is much more vulnerable, and it soon realizes that, but not Mossack Fonseca. Maunder said that their entire internet was behind a server. "Their web server was on the exact same network as their email servers based in Panama. They have been serving sensitive customer data from their portal website which includes a client login to access that data", he said.

In other words, Mossack Fonseca failed to take even the most basic actions to safeguard their confidential customer data. But even if they had put their internet server behind a firewall and separated it from their email servers, the Revolution Slider weakness could still have enabled attackers to get info on internal systems--it would simply have taken them somewhat more time to do so.

The most urgent cybersecurity task for any organization is to make sure that admins have applied all security patches to all software, not just the software that confronts the Internet. The plan you have in place for patching should be quick and thorough, but never count on all software to be properly patched. Fixed versions of the Revolution Slider as well as Drupal had long since been accessible, but Mossack Fonseca simply hadn't upgraded the software in their server.

Actually, obsolete versions of applications that a lot of organizations haven't properly patched are the most common cybersecurity vulnerability today. Simply because Mossack Fonseca's servers were behind by so much time since the original date made it especially egregious considering the sensitivity of their clients' information.

Automatic updates can cause a lot of specific problems, particularly in complex enterprise environments and other situations which require high availability. Updating web site software mechanically can break your site with no notice. Upgrades should not be done in a production environment. Upgrades should be sandboxed and analyzed before being added to the production servers.

While keeping the applications up-to-date is an essential defensive movement, organizations need to also play offense as well by minding their data lineage. Data lineage means understanding who has access to some data and if they have been granted access, very similar to the way law enforcement must handle proof. You must also understand what people do with your information and in particular how they're securing it. For the firms that trusted Mossack Fonseca using their private information, minding their information lineage was a significant weakness and a vulnerability that attackers were just too willing to exploit.

Adam Boone, CMO of safety vendor Certes Networks said that attacks on third parties like external law firms, builders, and the like are the main attack vector from the high-profile data breaches within the past three decades. He explains that an outside group, like a legal firm, also represents a path into the IT systems of the main enterprise target itself.

The following is one of the most important takeaways from the Mossack Fonseca violation: put your eggs in numerous baskets. Never give anyone access to any portion of your sensitive data. Furthermore, the more sensitive the information, the further you want to split the data up. In the corporate environment, such compartmentalization takes a new degree of segmentation technology. "Without modern access control and program isolation techniques, law firms are wide open for malicious insiders or outside attackers to get access to the most sensitive data," Boone clarifies the following is the final word of wisdom every organization should glean in the Mossack Fonseca debacle: always assume you have already been hacked, and that attackers can achieve at least a few of the goals before you shut them down. As a result, detecting the presence of hackers and cleaning up the messes they leave are significant, but always remember, the damage might have already been done.

Proper segmentation of your surroundings is your best approach to mitigating this harm. Clearly, if Mossack Fonseca had separated their internet server and email server from one another and from other private information, it would have been much more compartmentalized and so would have limited the damage. From the point of view of the law firm's customers, such segmentation is a more complex challenge. Every one of them should have guaranteed Mossack Fonseca had the proper protections in place, and they ought to also have split their confidential information across multiple law firms. The segmentation approach that is ideal for your organization may look different, but remember, odds are not all of your sensitive data will be locked away inside safe areas within your network. A lot of it may be in the cloud or in the hands of third parties. You can't stop all attacks from succeeding in these complex environments, but you can mitigate the harm through appropriate segmentation.

Ch. 5 Cyber Security Terms to Know

Antispyware Software

Anti-spyware software is deployed for the purpose of detecting, blocking, and/or removing spyware efforts. Spyware is a type of software that seeks to gather your personal information, without your consent. It has the capability to take over your computer completely! The information it collects is usually then sent to another party without your consent.

There 4 main different types of spyware:
- System monitors.
- Trojans.
- Adware.
- Tracking cookies.

Spyware is mainly used for tracking a user's movements online and sending to them many annoying and dangerous pop-up advertisements.

Here is how you can get infected:

Your system may get infected with spyware should you visit specific sites, by pop-up messages which ask you to obtain an application or program (told you they are evil!) through security holes in the browser or from other software, etc. Usually, spyware is well concealed. You might notice a spyware infection when the virus begins during startup of your computer along with your system's resources and slows it down in a way which will make you really, really, angry.

Antivirus Software

Antivirus software, sometimes called an anti-malware program (you can also call it AV for short), is computer software used to prevent, detect, and remove malicious applications. Antivirus protects your pc from a large number of dangers, including ransomware, rootkits, Trojans, spyware, phishing attacks or botnets.

Without getting technical, let's just say that the way antivirus scans for infections isn't actually coping with current threats. Their attacks can be vicious, so just bear in mind that an antivirus isn't always enough to protect your PC and you will need something more to keep you safe. But that does not mean you don't need an antivirus. YOU DO, trust me! However, you want other things too and I will tell you more about that later on. Normally, spyware is well concealed and it's also difficult to observe.

Cyber-Attack

Cyber-attack is classified as any type of offensive activity used by cyber criminals to deploy malicious code in your system with the goal of stealing, altering, destroying, or accepting any advantage from this activity. Cyber-attacks can target both people and things. ANYWHERE. ANYTIME. Individual customers, computer programs, information systems, IT infrastructure of all types and sizes - no one is safe! (And I'm not being dramatic about it.) And smarter cyber offenders launch stronger attacks, which lead to worse consequences.

Drive-by download

A drive-by download can refer to 2 things:

1. A download which you authorized but didn't understand the consequences. An example would be a download which installed an unknown or counterfeit executable program, ActiveX component, or Java applet without your knowledge.

2. The unintentional download of a virus (malware) onto your computer or mobile device without you being aware of it.

How you can get infected:

Drive-by downloads can happen many different ways. The most common way is when you visit a website or when you click on a pop-up window. These types of malicious downloads usually take advantage of a vulnerable browse or an operating system that is out of date and has a security flaw that has not been solved or patched. This is why it's crucial to constantly update your software.

Exploit

An exploit is a piece of software, a chunk of data, or a set of controls which takes advantage of a bug, glitch, or vulnerability for malicious purposes. Exploits may cause disruptions in the behavior of computer applications, hardware, or something electronic (usually computerized).

How you can get infected:

The most common way is again by clicking on a popup or visiting a website. By using exploits, cyber criminals can gain control of your computer. After that, they can do pretty much anything that they want. One of the ways to protect yourself from exploits is to update your software often.

Keylogging

Keylogging (also called keystroke logging) is a method that cyber criminals use to record (or log) the keys you strike on your keyboard in order to get passwords and other login information. Of course, they do this in a concealed manner so that you won't be aware of what they are doing. Always be aware that someone could be monitoring your keystrokes.

How you can get infected with a keylogger:
Keyloggers are usually used with malicious intentions, to steal passwords or credit card information. Although many anti-spyware applications can detect some software based keyloggers and quarantine them, disable or remove them, there is no solution that can claim to be 100% effective against this type of threat. It's import to always be aware of this.

Malvertising

Malvertising which is short for "malicious advertising", is the use of online advertising to spread malware. Cyber criminals inject malicious or malware-loaded code into online advertising networks or legitimate websites, which then infect your systems through clicking, redirection or drive-by downloads. Since online ads are managed by online advertising networks, even a legitimate website may host an infected web banner, although the website itself remains safe. There have even been many large websites that have unknowingly hosted malvertising such as The New York Times, the London Stock Exchange, Spotify, and The Onion.

How you can get infected:
Cyber criminals usually use pop-up ads, drive-by downloads, web widgets, hidden iframes, malicious banners, and/or third-party applications. An example of a third-party application would be forums, help desks, customer relationship management systems, etc. This is why malvertising is so wide-spread, affecting many users without their knowledge.

Malware

Malware (short for malicious software) is one of the terms you'll hear most often when it comes to cyber security threats. The term is used to describe any software used by cyber criminals to steal your information or to spy on your computer for a long time, without your knowledge. "Malware" is a general term used to refer to an entire category of malicious or intrusive software, including computer viruses, worms, Trojan horses, ransomware, spyware, adware, scareware, and other harmful programs.

How you can get infected:
Malware is usually spread through executable code, scripts, active content, and other software. The major threat it poses comes from malware being disguised as, or embedded in, non-malicious files, such as .jpeg, .mpeg, .exe, .gif, .mp3 and many, many more.

Patching

Patching is the process of updating software to another, newer version. A patch is a small update released by a software maker to fix bugs in existing applications. A patch may relate to usability and features but can also incorporate security features. Patching is important for your online safety because it prevents cyber criminals from launch attacks using Zero Day viruses.

Phishing

Phishing is just another method that cyber criminals use so as to acquire sensitive information like usernames, passwords, and credit card details (and sometimes money) by posing as a trusted entity in emails or other methods of digital communication. Phishing is a good example of social engineering methods used to deceive consumers and exploits the poor usability aspects of current web security technologies.

How you can get infected:
Phishing emails may look legitimate. They appear to come from your bank and may trick you into entering valid credentials on a fake website. Phishing is performed through emails, instant messaging programs or social networking posts such as Facebook, Twitter, LinkedIn, etc.

Ransomware

Ransomware is a form of malware that essentially holds something on a computer captive until a ransom is paid. This type of malware locks you out of your computer by either encrypting files on your hard drive or by locking down your system and displaying messages that try to extort you. The bad news is that the malware creator is the only one who knows the key to unlock your files.

How you can get infected:
Ransomware usually spreads like any other computer worm (by replicating itself in order to spread to other computers), and it could infect your computer through a downloaded
File. The chances of retrieving your data are close to impossible unless you're willing to pay the ransom. This is exactly why it's crucial to always have a back-up of your data in a secure location. Preferably off of the network that you're on. The bad guy will usually supply a program which can decrypt the files or send a decrypt code. Of course, you can't guarantee that paying the ransom will release the files.

Social engineering

Social engineering is one of the most commonly used methods of cyber hacking and it requires little to no technology. This attack is all about psychological manipulation used to persuade the victims to perform certain actions or divulge confidential information.

How you can become compromised:
For social engineering, criminals will use lies, impersonation, tricks, bribes, blackmail, and threats to attack information systems. Phishing is also a form of social engineering. A good example of this would be to imagine a criminal posing as a contractor, exterminator, fire marshal, or technician to go unnoticed as they steal your secrets or trick you into giving them personal information about yourself or your company.

Spam

We all know that spam is made of those annoying, unsolicited emails that clog our inboxes. But lately, spam has spread to instant messaging apps, texting, blogs, forums, search engines, file sharing and social media.

How you can get infected:
While spam itself may not seem very dangerous, it can sometimes carry malware, spread viruses, worms, and other types of threats, such as financial theft, identity theft, data and intellectual property theft, fraud, and deceptive marketing.

Trojan (Trojan horse)

A Trojan horse (normally referred to as a Trojan) is a kind of malware that hides itself as a normal file or program to fool you into downloading and installing malware. A Trojan can do any number of dangerous things to your system, such as give cyber offenders some unauthorized, remote access to your infected computer. Once that occurs, cyber criminals can steal information (logins, fiscal data, or digital money), install more malware, and modify files, monitor your action (screen viewing, keylogging, etc.), use the pc in botnets (a collection of Internet-connected apps communicating with other similar apps so as to distribute malware), encrypt your files, like in the instance of ransomware, crash your computer, format your disks destroying all of the contents on your device, etc..

How you can get infected:
Of course, there are many ways in which your system can become infected by a Trojan. Here are only a few:
- Through email attachments.
- Software or music downloads.
- Unsafe instant messages.
- Peer 2 peer downloads.

- Routine forms that need to be filled in.
- Drive-by downloads, etc.

URL or web content filtering

URL or web filtering technologies is software that keeps you from accessing inappropriate websites or content or that prevents you from ending up in a harmful web place (and by dangerous I'm talking about malware-laden). The program's filter assesses the origin or content of a web page against a set of guidelines supplied by the business or person that has set up the URL filter. If the webpage has been blacklisted or marked as infected, it is going to deny access to that web location and might block an attack.

Virus (Computer Virus)

A computer virus (normally just called virus) is a type of malware capable of replicating itself and spreading to other servers and data files. Viruses spread to other computers by attaching themselves to different applications and executing code when you launch any of those infected programs. But they're really sneaky, so they can also distribute through script files and cross-site scripting vulnerabilities in web apps. Viruses are also very dangerous because they are sometimes used to steal information, harm your computers, log keystrokes, create botnets, spam your contacts, steal your money, display amusing or political messages on your display (probably the least of your concerns), and more.

How you can get infected:
Viruses install themselves without your consent since cyber criminals utilize social technologies and exploit software bugs and vulnerabilities to access your computing tools. Viruses can live in executable files (.exe or .com files), in data documents (Microsoft Word documents or PDFs), or in the boot sector of the hard disk. Or within a mix of all these. And the worst part is that some viruses are polymorphic, meaning that the virus has no parts which

remain identical between infections, making it rather hard to detect directly with an antivirus solution which is only comparing virus definitions and not looking at heuristics as well.

Vulnerability

A cyber security vulnerability is a weakness which allows an individual to undermine your system's data security defenses. A vulnerability may appear in various forms. An example is your Java software has not been updated to the latest version. This also gives an attacker access to this defect. A vulnerability is simply a pretense a cyber-criminal can use to establish a complete scale assault on your system. He still needs the proper tools for this, but they come in a massive supply online and they are cheap as well. The way to guard yourself from vulnerabilities is to keep your software updated at all times.

Zero-Day virus

Now that you know exactly what a vulnerability is, it'll be really easy to understand what a Zero-Day virus is also. Zero-Day viruses occur when a flaw is discovered for the first time in a piece of software. They exploit that vulnerability immediately, starting an assault which users can't defend themselves against for two simple reasons. The defect is exploited by launching a previously unknown computer virus or other malware. Antivirus programs rely upon signatures to spot malware, but the signature for this new breed of virus or malware is not in their database, because it's new and has not been sampled. That is why antivirus software is not effective against Zero-Day viruses, and also that is why you require additional solutions to guard you from advanced attacks such as these.

How you can get infected:
- Drive-by downloads.
- Malvertising.

- Spam.
- Through email attachments.
- Software or music downloads.
- Unsafe instant messages.
- Peer 2 peer downloads.
- Normal looking forms that need to be filled in, etc.

The main difference is that once you get infected, there's not much that you can do to stop the infection and mitigate its effects.

Ch. 6 Passwords

Would it take 2 Minutes or 100,000 Years for your password to be hacked? Most of us know powerful passwords are key to private and corporate security. But managing passwords is a pain. In fact, many IT service management professionals can tell you it is the most common cause end users call the help desk for. This is not surprising considering that most business users possess at least eight passwords they utilize on a daily basis to log into a multitude of systems and devices. Management and senior level executives can juggle upwards of 25, based on their function and level of access.

The Worst Passwords

Each year, a list of the most frequently used passwords is released. Time after time we see the expected ones; "password", "qwerty", and "1234567890". Amusingly, popular new passwords often pop up with regard to pop-culture. A report from 2020 indicates a surge in Starwars themed words with "starwars", "solo", "Lady", all landing on the list for last year.

Here is a list of the top 25 worst password from 2020,

according to Splashdata, with their 2019 ranking in brackets:

1. 123456 (Unchanged)
2. password (Unchanged)
3. 12345678 (Up 1)
4. qwerty (Up 1)
5. 12345 (Down 2)
6. 123456789 (Unchanged)
7. football (Up 3)
8. 1234 (Down 1)
9. 1234567 (Up 2)
10. baseball (Down 2)
11. welcome (New)
12. 1234567890 (New)
13. abc123 (Up 1)
14. 111111 (Up 1)
15. 1qaz2wsx (New)
16. dragon (Down 7)
17. master (Up 2)
18. monkey (Down 6)
19. letmein (Down 6)
20. login (New)
21. princess (New)
22. qwertyuiop (New)
23. solo (New)
24. passw0rd (New)
25. starwars (New)

The Perfect Password

So, how do you create the ideal password? Experts advocate creating something long, random, and hard to imagine. Use a combination of symbols, figures, and letters such as lower and upper cases. It's also important not to use the exact same password over and over again. Consider this. A 6-character password that contains only lowercase letters will probably take approximately 10 minutes to get an experienced hacker to crack. A 9-character password that combines letters, symbols, and numbers would take over 44,000 decades. Wow. If you're having a hard time creating the ideal password on your own, opt for a password generator. They are free, fast, and easy-to-use.

Explore Your Options

It is no wonder so many calls are pouring into the service Desk in regard to password management. The great news is the fact that most organizations can fix the password management dilemma with self-service password reset options. It is quite simple to calculate the ROI of these tools when you've got a general idea of the quantity of calls associated with passwords you generally receive and the average price of a level 1 incident (which is typically around $25/30).

If you're currently replacing or researching self-service password reset solutions, contemplate INVICTAPass. A password management tool for organizations of all sizes, INVICTAPass is easy to configure, manage and deploy. With their customized automatic registration process users normally get upwards of 90% adoption rate, crucial to the achievement of almost any password reset tool.

You shouldn't keep your passwords in a text file, spreadsheet, plain text or a similar, unprotected document! Why? I would not like to see you scramble to change 200 passwords as soon as possible if you got hacked. You shouldn't utilize the default password sent to you by a service supplier! Why? It's simple: because those passwords are usually straightforward and, consequently, easily breakable. It would be like giving candy to a baby, just like they say. And cyber criminals love both the passwords and (likely) candy.

You should not use one of the shamefully weak passwords recorded on this top 25 listed before! You should not use words which can be found in a dictionary or which are common phrases! Why? Because cyber criminals have a strategy known as "dictionary attack". A dictionary attack is based on trying all of the strings at a pre-arranged listing, normally derived from a list of phrases taken out of a dictionary (hence the name). And dictionary attacks frequently triumph, exactly because a lot of people use short passwords which include ordinary phrases or simple variants by simply adding a digit or punctuation character.

You shouldn't use passwords that include your birthday or other information that's readily available online! Why? Because tracking down your own personal information online is the thing that gives cyber criminals an entrance. Even in the event that you have all of your privacy preferences pushed to the maximum, there's always a way around them. You should not use the identical password without changing it for a long time period! Why? Because passwords, exactly like the ice-cream in your refrigerator, have an expiry date. An old password may be easy to crack and there is a lot that can go downhill from that point.

You shouldn't use the identical password twice! This is a big one. Seriously! Why? This really is one of the major mistakes most of us make when it comes to password management. Using the identical password for more than 1 account (and generally making it a simple one) means that cyber criminals will access MORE accounts at once, and they will have the ability to steal MORE data and do MORE damage!

Ch. 7 Business Email Compromise

It's ruined the careers of lots of executives and loyal workers. Successful CEOs are fired because of it. Stock prices have dropped because of it. IPOs and mergers are removed from the table. Known as CEO fraud or Business Email Compromise (BEC), the FBI reports that this type of cyber-crime generated over 23,000 complaints which were accountable for losses of more than $1.7 billion in 2019 alone. Therefore, any organization headed by its CEO must immediately learn to integrate the skills and technologies used to prevent BEC into daily operations -- or face the consequences. This CEO fraud prevention chapter provides a comprehensive summary of how to cope with this growing wave of preventable cyber-crime.

What is CEO Fraud? The FBI refers to it as Company Email Compromise (BEC) or Email Account Compromise (EAC) and defines it as "a complicated scam that targets both companies and those who perform valid transfer-of-funds requests. The scam is frequently carried out when a subject compromises legitimate companies or personal email accounts through social engineering or computer intrusion to run unauthorized transfers of funds."

CEO fraud is just another name for this type of scam and it usually involves tricking someone from a company into making a massive cable transfer into what turns out to be a fake account, redirecting paycheck deposits or perhaps asking employees' Personally Identifiable Information (PII) or for Wage and Tax Statement (W-2) forms.

Most sufferers are in the U.S. (all 50 states), however, associations in 177 other countries have also reported incidents. While the deceptive transfers have been sent to at least 140 nations, most end up in China and Hong Kong. Unless the fraud is spotted within 24 hours, the odds of recovery are modest at best.

Certainly, large enterprises are a lucrative target. But tiny businesses are equally likely to be targeted. Apart from being a company which engages in cable transfers, there is no discernible pattern concerning a focus on a particular sector or type of company. The bad guys do not discriminate. Fortunately, organizations can learn/familiarize themselves with all of the different approaches in which these attacks have been initiated.

Phishing

Phishing emails are sent to large numbers of users simultaneously in an effort to "fish" for sensitive information by posing as a trusted resource --frequently with legitimate-looking trademarks attached. Banks, credit card providers, delivery firms, law enforcement, along with the IRS are a few of the common ones. A phishing effort typically shoots out emails to huge numbers of users. Most of them are shipped to people who don't use that lender, for example, but by sheer weight of numbers, these emails will make their way to a certain proportion of likely candidates.

Spear Phishing

This is a more concentrated form of phishing. The cyber-criminal has studied up on the a particular group and has gleaned data from various social networking websites which is then used to con users to help them formulate a more personalized attack. The email generally goes to a single individual or a small group of individuals who use this lender or service. Some form of personalization is included -- possibly the individual's name, or the name of a client.

Executive Whaling

Here, the bad guys target top executives and administrators, generally to siphon off money from accounts or steal confidential data. Personalization and in depth understanding of the executive and the business are the hallmarks of this kind of fraud.

Social Engineering

All of these techniques fall under the broader category of social engineering. This benign sounding label was initially defined as the application of sociological principles to particular societal problems. But within a security context, it has come to signify the use of psychological manipulation to fool people into divulging private info or providing access to capital. The art of social engineering often includes mining data from social networking sites that are collecting something named Open-Source Intelligence (OSINT). LinkedIn, Facebook, and other sites provide a plethora of information about organizational employees which may be used to craft attacks. This may include their contact information, relations, friends, continuing business deals and much more.

Regrettably, these scams have a higher rate of success. The Verizon 2020 Data Breach Investigations Report (DBIR) demonstrated that phishing unsurprisingly topped the record for high hazard activities in breaches. While phishing emails might not directly cause CEO fraud, they're the best avenue of entrance for malware and spyware into the enterprise. Once indoors, cyber offenders can bide their time finding the financial interactions and connections within the organization. They finally learn enough to spring a persuasive BEC assault, usually posing as a company executive or an account personnel. They can sit unobserved for months while they examine the essential people, processes, procedures, and protocols necessary to perform wire transfers or other fiscal redirection within that business environment.

The FBI decided that there are five main scenarios by which this scam is utilized:

1. Business working with a foreign supplier: This scam takes advantage of a long-standing wire-transfer relationship with a supplier but asks for the funds to be sent to a different account.

2. Business receiving or initiating a wire transfer request: By compromising the email accounts of top executives, another employee receives a message to transfer funds somewhere, or a financial institution gets a request from someone to send money to another account. These requests appear genuine because they come from the correct email address.

3. Business contacts receiving fraudulent correspondence: By taking over an employee's email account and sending invoices out to organization suppliers, money is transferred to bogus accounts.

4. Executive and attorney impersonation: The fraudsters pretend to be lawyers or executives dealing with confidential and time-sensitive matters.

5. Data theft: Fraudulent e-mails request either all wage or tax statement (W-2) forms or an organization list of personally identifiable information (PII). These come from compromised and/or spoofed executive email accounts and are sent to the HR department, auditing departments or other accounts.

These kind of attacks are not rare at all. In fact, they are so successful that billions are being stolen every year using this method. Here are a few examples of some attacks:

Israeli Startup and a VC Company: Bad actors were able to compromise the email accounts of an Israeli startup company, then redirected email messages into look-alike domain names for both the Venture Capital Company along with the startup, and walked off with $1 million in startup seed money. This is a brilliant man-in-the-middle attack that was successful since the attackers generated fake domains with an extra letter in the address at the conclusion and tricked both sides to routing emails via the attackers' servers.

Two B.C. law firms: 2 B.C. law firms dropped almost $2 million to attackers who sent emails to the firms asking that funds transfers move to various accounts. All these were performed through spoofed email addresses that were either the same as the sender or only off by a single letter.

Two defense contractors and a university: Two defense contractors and a university lost roughly $170,000 in three events where an attacker impersonated employees at a university. The attacker ordered expensive electronic measurement tools and billed the university. It was a very simple scam. They utilized spoofed email addresses which faked being the university and obtained fraudulent lines of credit to easily make the purchases. In many of the publicly disclosed cases, funds have been retrieved due to rapid reporting and identification by employees. But this insight might provide a false impression given that the FBI says that overall losses are well into the billions. Beyond the immediate capital looted, the indirect harm due to CEO fraud is additionally substantial. C-level executives are fired, reputations are ruined, and shares can take a hammering.

Of course, the CEO is not the only one in the organization that the criminals will use. In addition, the HR team, IT manager, C-level positions, other senior executives, and anyone with finance approval is likely to be on the receiving end of one of these attacks, using the authority of the CEO as leverage.

Finance: The finance department is especially vulnerable in organizations that frequently engage in large wire transfers. Frequently, sloppy internal policies simply require an email from your CEO or other senior person to initiate the transfer. Cyber criminals usually obtain entrance via phishing and spend a few months doing recon and formulating a plan. They mirror the typical wire transfer authorization protocols, hijack a relevant email account, and send the request to the proper individual in fund to transmit the money.

In addition to the CFO, this may be done via the identity of anyone in accounts that is authorized to transfer money.

HR: Human Resources signifies a wonderfully open street to the contemporary enterprise. After all, this section has access to each individual in the business, manages the worker database, and is in charge of recruitment. Therefore, a major function of HR would be to hold résumés from tens of thousands of potential applicants. All the cyber offenders will need to do is include spyware inside a résumé and they can surreptitiously start their secret data gathering activities.

Additionally, W-2 and PII scams are becoming more commonplace. HR receives requests from spoofed mails and ends up sending employee information such as social security numbers and employee email addresses to criminal associations.

Executive Team: Each member of the executive team could be thought of as a high-value target. Many possess some kind of financial authority. If their email accounts are hacked, then it generally provides cyber criminals access to all sorts of confidential information, not to mention intelligence about types of prospective ongoing deals. Hence executive accounts should receive particular attention from a safety standpoint.

IT: The IT director and IT personnel with authority over access controllers, password management and email accounts are much greater high-value targets. In the case that their credentials are hacked or phished, hackers will gain entrance to every part of the company. Virus and malware protection has long been seen as only an IT duty. However, the events of recent decades have emphasized the threat of having this viewpoint. With the FBI warning corporations that they are in danger and so many high-profile victims in the news, associations, headed by their CEO, must incorporate cyber-risk management into day-to-day operations.

Furthermore, organizations must take reasonable measures to prevent cyber-incidents and mitigate the impact of inevitable breaches. Many federal and state laws in the USA, Australia, and other countries use the concept of acting "reasonably". Blaming something on IT or even a member of staff isn't a defense. CEOs are responsible for restoring normal operations after a data breach and ensuring an organization's assets and organization's reputation are both protected. Failure to do this can open the door to legal action. Let's put it another way. A cyber breach might cause the loss of a bidding on a large contract, could compromise intellectual property (IP), and a reduction of earnings, to mention only a few of those consequences.

These challenges put cybersecurity firmly on peak of the organizational chart, very similar to other kinds of corporate threats. Technology is critical, but we must check our people and processes. "Social engineering is a form of hacking that uses influence strategies." - Kevin Mitnick

Most attempts towards risk mitigation concentrate on technologies. Similarly, proper backup and disaster recovery (DR) procedures must be in place. For example, a 3-2-1 backup strategy (three copies of the data, on two distinct types of media, with one off site) is a wise practice along with testing of the restore function on a regular basis.

Nonetheless, these technology safeguards must be encouraged by what is called the individual firewall -- an internal team that is educated on cyber threats that may put a phishing email a mile off, fast report it, and won't fall prey to CEO fraud. The best way to handle this problem is new-school security awareness training. Thousands of organizations are doing so with fantastic results. Educating users by means of this training makes it much more difficult for them to fall victim to social engineering attacks. Establishing a human firewall will not remove breaches completely, but it is going to decrease them.

1. Prevention: Many steps need to dovetail closely together within an effective prevention program. It's essential to be able to spot High-Risk Users. Impose more controls and safeguards in those areas of the organization. For example, on fund approvals for wire transfers, stipulate several factors of authorization and a time interval that needs to elapse before the transfer is implemented. It is a good idea to run a search of all high-risk users to see how vulnerable they are. For instance, LinkedIn and Facebook profiles often provide comprehensive personal information or even what could be considered sensitive company data like the person having wire transfer authority, in addition to email addresses and lists of relations.

2. Technical Controls: Various technical controls must be instituted to stop the advancement of phishing attacks. Email filtering is the first level of defense, but it is far from foolproof. Authentication measures must be resolved. Rather than a simple username and password, which the bad guys have a fantastic success rate of getting past, two factor authentication also needs something which only the user owns, such as a physical token. This makes it considerably more difficult for potential intruders to gain access and steal that person's individual identity or data. Key fobs, access cards, and sending a code to a documented mobile phone are some of the potential prevention methods, but I favor the Google authentication app. Automated password and user ID policy authorities is another wise defense. Comprehensive access and password management can also minimize malware and ransomware outbreaks and successful email account takeovers. Take a look at existing technical controls and do something to plug any gaps that you find.

3. Policy: Every company should set security policy, review it regularly for gaps, publish it and also make sure employees follow it. It must include such matters as employees not opening attachments or clicking on hyperlinks from an unknown source, not using USB drives on office computers, password management policy (not using the same passwords on other sites or machines, no post-it notes on displays as password reminders), completing specific kinds of security training, including training on security coverage, and the list of other dangers to employee in order to create a total security education plan. Policy on Wi-Fi access, for example, ought to be clearly understood. Include vendors and contractors as part of this group if they want wireless access when onsite. Policy also needs to exist on wire transfers and about the handling of confidential data. It should never be possible to get a cyber-criminal to hijack a corporate email accounts and convince a person to move a large sum of money immediately. Policy should limit such transactions to relatively tiny quantities. Anything outside a predetermined threshold needs to require further authorizations. Similarly, with confidential information such as IP or employee documents, policy should determine a chain of approvals before such information is published.

4. Procedures: IT should have measures in place to block sites known to disperse ransomware, maintain software patches and virus signature files up to date, carry out vulnerability scanning and self-assessment using best practice frameworks such as US-CERT or SANS Institute guidelines, and also conduct regular penetration tests on Wi-Fi and other networks to see exactly how easy it is to obtain entrance. These and many other security processes will go a long way toward protecting your organization. Procedures must also be developed to stop CEO fraud and BEC. Wire transfer authorization is one situation requiring careful consideration. Set this up in a way that any wire transfer necessitates more than one authorization, as well as a confirmation beyond email. Phone, or face-to-face affirmation, should be included. If by phone, just use a preexisting number for your contact, none given to you in an email address. The subject of time also needs to be part of process. To guard against urgency injected by a cyber-criminal into an email, regular procedure should call for a 24-hour waiting period before funds are transferred. This gives ample time for the necessary authorizations and side-checks for credibility to be finished.

5. Cyber-Risk Planning: Cybersecurity has been treated as a technology issue. However, cyber threat must be handled at the most senior level in precisely the exact same fashion as other important corporate risks. The CEO must completely understand the company's cyber risks, its plan to handle those risks, and also the answer plan for when the inevitable violation happens. CEOs also should consider the risk to the organization's reputation as well as the legal exposure that could result from a cyber-incident. CEO fraud has to be a part of this risk management evaluation. While this assessment is of a technical character, it's more about organizational processes. Executive leadership has to be educated about the current amount of risk and its possible business impact. This is seldom true within organizations which constantly face phishing and CEO fraud. Management must know the quantity of cyber incidents discovered per week and of what type. Policy should be established that summarizes thresholds and types of events that need reporting to administration. In the event of an outbreak, a strategy has to be set up to address identified risks. This is just another weak point in many organizations, nevertheless it's an essential element of preserving the integrity of information on the network.

Best practices and industry standards should be assembled and used to review the present cybersecurity program. Revise the program according to a thorough evaluation. Another facet of this is routine testing of the cyber-incident response plan. Run a test of a simulated breach to see how well the company performs. Augment the program based on outcomes. Finally, call your insurance carrier and go over the fine print regarding your coverage. If no cyber protection exists, acquire it rapidly. Go over the details of cybersecurity insurance to make sure it covers the many types of information breaches and includes the several types of CEO fraud and BEC strikes.

6. Training: No matter how great your prevention steps are, not all breaches are unavoidable. But user instruction plays a big part in reducing the threat. Make it a key aspect of your prevention plan. Start by training staff on security policy. Augment this by producing a very simple handbook on the fundamentals of security. This should include reminders never to add USB drives from outside devices into machines. It also needs to examine password management, such rather than devoting work passwords on other sites or machines. Phishing needs its own training and instruction, as it represents one of the biggest dangers. Instruct users that hovering over email addresses and links in messages shows the actual email address or destination URL. Just because it states "Bank of America," or "IT department" with all the right logos does not mean it is from this origin. Insert further instruction not to open unknown file types, click on links, or open attachments from unknown people or entities. If, for instance, educating a student body in this manner is not feasible, set them on a separate network and severely restrict their access to sensitive information. There are many programs which monitor click speeds on phishing emails and it's possible to exploit user education to bring that number down. But don't expect 100 percent success. Good employee education can reduce phishing success significantly and offer valuable threat intellect through reporting, but it will not take it down to zero. There is always someone who doesn't pay attention, is in a rush that day, or can still be outsmarted with a clever cyber-criminal. Comprehensive data security best practices also have to be enforced.

7. Simulated Phishing: The initial simulation establishes a baseline number of users who are phish-prone. Continue simulated phishing attacks at least once each month, but twice is greater. Once users know that they will be analyzed on a regular basis and that there are consequences for repeated fails, behavior changes. They develop a less trusting mindset and get far better at seeing a scam email. Phishing tests should not be sent out to all workers with the same text. In cases like this, one employee spots it and leans out of the cubicle to warn others. Instead, send several types of emails to small collections of consumers and randomize the information and times they are sent.

8. Red Flags: Security awareness training should incorporate teaching people to watch out for red flags. In emails, for example, look for awkward wording and misspelling. Be alert to slight alterations of business names, for example "Centriffy" instead of "Centrify" or even "Tilllage" rather than "Tillage". Hackers have become very good at producing spoofed email addresses and URLs that are extremely close to actual company addresses, but only slightly different. Another red flag is abrupt urgency or time-sensitive issues. Scammers typically manufacture some rush factor or alternative that may manipulate reliable staff to act rapidly. Phrases such as "cut to admin expenses," "pressing wire transfer," "urgent invoice payment" and "fresh account information" are frequently used, according to the FBI. Whenever an email or text message causes a powerful emotional response, it needs to be treated with extra scrutiny. This is vital because cyber offenders use emotions to cloud critical thinking.

Should a CEO fraud incident take place, there are immediate steps that should be taken:

1. Contact your bank immediately: Inform them of the cable transfer in question. Give them full details of the amount, the account's destination, and any other pertinent information. Request the name of the lender if it's likely to remember the transfer. Get in contact with the cybersecurity section of the bank, brief them about the incident and ask for their intervention. They can contact their counterparts in the foreign exchange to get them to stop the money from being pulled or transferred elsewhere.

2. Contact your attorneys: In some cases, especially in

case of a significant reduction, communications might need to be sent out to shareholders and stakeholders, and regulations might require reporting of this incident within a certain timeframe. Your attorneys may provide advice on next steps of action, help prepare a telling statement if necessary, and assist in navigating regulatory and insurance processes.

3. Contact law enforcement: Information: Description of this incident and consider providing the following monetary information to return or freeze the funds. When from the U.S., the local FBI office is where to get started. The FBI, working with the local law enforcement, may be able to freeze the funds. This is the important information the law enforcement may need:

• Originating Name
• Originating Location
• Originating Bank Name
• Originating Bank Account Number
• Recipient Name
• Recipient Bank Name
• Recipient Bank Account Number
• Recipient Bank Location (if available)
• Intermediary Bank Name (if available)
• SWIFT Number.
• Date.
• Amount of Transaction.
• Additional Information if it exists.

4. File a complaint: Victims should stop by and file a complaint regardless of dollar reduction or time lost. The place to file is in the www.IC3.gov site. In addition to the financial information and the bullet points in the previous paragraph, victims must also provide these descriptors if known:

• IP and/or email address of fraudulent email
• Date and time of incidents
• Incorrectly formatted invoices or letterheads
• Requests for secrecy or immediate action

• Strange timing, unexpected requests, or wording of the fraudulent phone calls or emails

• Phone numbers of the fraudulent phone calls

• Describe any and all phone contacts to include frequency and timing of calls

• Foreign accents of the callers

• Poorly worded or grammatically incorrect emails

• Reports of any previous email phishing activity

5. Brief the board and senior management: Call a crisis meeting to brief the board and senior management about the episode, measures taken, and additional actions to be completed.

6. Conduct IT forensics: Have IT investigate the breach to find the attack vector. If an executive email was compromised, take instant action to recover control of this account, such as changing the password and recovering any email addresses that were modified by the attackers. But don't stop there. It is very likely that the organization has been further infiltrated and other areas have been compromised. Have them run a comprehensive list of detection technologies to get any and all malware which may be lurking and waiting to attack again.

7. Contact your insurance company: Once gone, in most cases, funds cannot be recovered. This is particularly true when the victim does not move quickly. Therefore, it is necessary to speak to your insurance company to discover when you're insured for the attack. While many businesses have taken out cyber insurance, not all are insured in case of CEO fraud. This is a gray area in insurance and many refuse to pay up. A lot of men and women who've reported CEO fraud to their insurer find this kind of incident isn't covered.

Regardless of the presence of a specific cyber insurance policy, the unfortunate fact is that no hardware or software was hacked. It was the human that was hacked instead. Insurance companies draw a distinction between monetary instruments and email fraud. Many businesses are covered in case of a fraudulent financial tool. However, CEO fraud can be categorized differently. It is looked upon by some insurance companies as being purely an email fraud rather than a monetary instrument fraud. In other words, it's being regarded in several cases as a matter of internal neglect or email impersonation as opposed to being a financial crime tool. Nevertheless, there are scores of carriers in the market providing up to $300 million in coverage. Coverage extensions have developed to include both the third-party liability and first-party cost and expenses associated with a data breach or cyber assault. Even if the insurance carrier isn't eager to pay instantly, they could have resources available. These resources might include security experts on retainer, who can help execute forensics and make certain that the attackers are out of the company's networks.

8. Bring in outside security specialists: If the organization has been broken into, it must mean there are deficiencies in the existing technology safeguards. These can prove very difficult for IT to see. Therefore, bringing in outside help to discover some area of intrusion that IT might have missed makes a lot of sense. The goal is to remove all malware which could possibly be buried in the current systems. The bad guys are inside the company and the organization isn't safe until the attack vector is dispersed and all traces of the assault have been eradicated. This is not a simple task. Remember that your insurance company might have recommended groups or resources available that could be insured completely or offered with a discount through them. So, be sure to ask your insurance company before hiring a security specialist.

9. Isolate security policy violations: For such an incident to happen, there is likely to be signs of violations of existing policy. Conduct an internal evaluation to cover these offenses and to remove any possibility of collusion with the criminals. Simply take the appropriate disciplinary action.

10. Make a plan to remedy security deficiencies: Once the immediate results of the attack have been addressed and full data was gathered about it, make a plan that includes adding staff and technology training to protect against the exact same sort of episode from repeating. As a very important part of this, be sure to beef up staff awareness training.

Conclusion: There is not any substitute for preparation in regards to coping with cyber criminals and the many flavors of CEO fraud. The CEO fraud prevention examples given here will direct you through essential actions to take to teach the organization how to prevent this type of attack. While these steps will significantly decrease the likelihood of an attack, all it takes is just one gullible or inattentive user to allow the bad guys inside. In such instances where CEO fraud has been perpetrated, the CEO fraud response recommendations apply.

Security awareness training is an essential part in making a human firewall around your business. Just when users are fully aware of the many facets of phishing will they be capable of withstanding even the most complex efforts at CEO fraud.

Ch. 8 IT Disasters You Can Avoid

IT mistakes within an organization, even when using bleeding edge technology, can result in cost overruns, missed deadlines, and sometimes, can get you fired. Here's a list of top disasters it is possible to avoid with tips from experts.

Overzealous password policies: A very clear and consistently enforced password policy is vital for any network. What good is a firewall when an attacker just needs to type "password" to get in? But strict password safety cuts both ways. If your password demands are excessively intricate and draconian, or if users are forced to change their passwords too often, your policy can have the opposite of its intended effect. Users pushed to the limit of remembering passwords end up writing them down - in a drawer, on a Post-It, or onto a piece of tape stuck on their notebook keyboard. Don't undermine the ultimate aim of your password coverage by focusing on unrealistic requirements. Besides, passwords are so 2010. If you want strict access control now, think multifactor authentication.

Mismanaging the datacenter: System administrators aren't exactly famous for their neatness, but at the datacenter, order is essential. Spaghetti cabling, mislabeled racks, and legacy gear no longer being used can all cause big problems. Careless provisioning can quickly direct an admin to reconfigure the incorrect machine or reformat the wrong volume. Therefore, we need to keep things clean (and always double-check your log-ins). Good systems housekeeping also entails getting manufacturing servers off engineers' desks and out of the hiding places in the cellar. Managing those assets is IT's job, and it should shoulder the load of diligence with gusto. Make sure your CFO knows the importance of maintaining a datacenter that is large and well-equipped enough to scale with the company without ever turning into a jungle.

Losing control over critical IT assets: Senior management has a request: "The advertising team needs to run ad-hoc SQL queries against the production database". It is easy enough to implement, so you grudgingly allow it to happen and move on. The next thing you know, poorly formed questions are bringing the server to its knees before each Thursday's advertising meeting. Your next assignment? "Fix the performance problem". Backseat drivers are a danger; but handing over the keys to somebody who can't drive can be deadly. The experience and judgment of IT management plays a crucial role in all decisions related to IT assets. Do not abdicate that responsibility from a desire to avoid confrontation. A bad idea is a bad idea, even though company managers do not realize it.

Treating "legacy" as a dirty word: Eager young techies may hate the concept that mission-critical processes are still running on systems their grandparents' age, but there's often very good reason for IT to have an appreciation for age over attractiveness. Screen-scraping (copying information that shows on a digital display so it can be used for another purpose) isn't as hot as SOA (service-oriented architecture), but an older system that runs reliably is less risky than a brand-new unknown. Modernizing legacy systems can be expensive, too. By way of instance, the State of California hopes to spend US$177 million on a revamped payroll system. And based on one IDC study, annual maintenance costs for new applications jobs typically run into the millions. In these days of tightened IT budgets, don't be in too much of a hurry to make your "dinosaurs" extinct before it's their time to go.

Ignoring the human element of security: Responsibility is something which every employee needs to share. Make users aware of prospective social engineering attacks, the dangers involved, and how they undermine security. For instance, by giving away passwords. Kevin Mitnick (from chapter one) is fond of saying, "the weakest link in any network is its people."

The most fortified system is still vulnerable if users can be tricked into undermining it. In this age of phishing and identity theft, safety can be compromised by simply giving confidential information over the phone. As of this writing, network admins have access to a broad collection of security tools. However, ask any hacker and they'll say that because of this reason, user education ought to be the cornerstone of your website security policy.

Creating indispensable employees: As reassuring as it may be to understand that a single employee knows your systems inside and outside, it's never in a firm's best interests to let IT workers become really crucial. Take, as an instance, former City of San Francisco worker Terry Childs that was finally jailed for refusing to disclose key network passwords which only he knew. In addition, employees who are too valuable in particular roles may also get passed up for career improvement and miss out on new opportunities.

Rather than building specialized superstars, you need to encourage collaboration and train your staff to work with a variety of projects and teams. A multi-talented, diverse workforce in the IT department will not only be happier, it's going to be better for business, too.

Raising issues instead of offering solutions: Are all of your warnings about critical vulnerabilities falling on deaf ears? Identifying security risks and possible points of failure is a significant part of IT management, but the job does not end there. Problems with no obvious solutions will only make senior management defensive and dismissive. Before reporting a problem, formulate a concrete plan of actions to tackle it, then present both at precisely the same time. To win support for your plan, always clarify your concerns about business risk - and have information available to support your case. You ought to be able to say not only exactly what it will cost to resolve the problem, but also what it may cost if it doesn't get fixed.

Logging in as root: One of the oldest rookie mistakes remains alive and well in 2021. Techs who routinely log in to the administrator or "root" accounts for minor tasks run the risk of wiping out valuable data or even whole systems. Fortunately, modern operating systems - including Mac OS 11, Ubuntu, and Windows 10 - have taken steps to curb this practice, by shipping with the highest-level privileges disabled by default. Rather than running as root all the time, techs should enter the administrative password only on occasions where they need to execute a significant systems maintenance task. It might be a hassle, but it is just good practice. It is high time that every IT worker started doing this.

Teetering on the bleeding edge: With public beta applications now commonplace, there exists great temptation to only rely on cutting-edge tools in production environments. Resist it. Enterprise IT ought to be about finding answers, not keeping up with the Joneses. It's OK to be an early adopter on your desktop computer, but the datacenter is no place to gamble. Rather, choose a measured approach. Keep abreast of the latest developments, but don't deploy new tools for production use until you've given them a thorough road test, possibly in a sandbox environment first. Experiment with pilot projects at the departmental level. Also, make sure outside support can be obtained. You do not want to be left on your own if the latest and greatest turns out to be ready for prime time.

Reinventing the wheel: There is no better way to ensure IT viability than to take charge of your own applications requirements. But too often, companies employ software developers simply to squander their abilities on the wrong jobs. For example, you wouldn't want to create your own Web browser or relational database. Why, then, do so many businesses waste energy building custom CRM (customer relationship manager) programs or content management techniques, when innumerable high-quality products exist to fulfill those needs? For In-house software development projects, we should be creating only that which can confer competitive advantage. Functions which aren't unique to your company are best managed with off-the-shelf applications. Failing that, start with an open-source project and tweak it to meet your own requirements. Redundant development jobs only distract from genuine business objectives.

Losing track of mobile users: Networked tools make it easy to push security updates, run nightly backups, and even handle software installation for users across an entire business - provided, of course, that their PCs are linked to the corporate LAN. But what about consumers who spend most of their time off-site? Mobility and telecommuting in 2021 have changed the sport for systems management, network security, and business continuity. Files that are never backed up can mean hundreds of hours of lost productivity. And what will happen to your sensitive data in case of theft? Automated IT policies provide no reassurance if street warriors can slip through the cracks.

Falling into the compliance money-pit: If it comes to complying with Sarbanes-Oxley, HIPAA, and other regulations, too many companies fall back to the Band-Aid method. But throwing money at nebulous compliance objectives just drains funds that might otherwise be used for more tangible projects.

While a critical regulatory deadline may necessitate a fast compliance fix sometimes, it is ideal to choose a holistic approach. If planning your compliance plan, think in terms of global policies and procedures, rather than point solutions targeted at specific clauses. Aim to remove redundant processes and manual record keeping and concentrate on ways to automate the compliance process on a continuous basis. To do otherwise is simply throwing good money after bad.

Underestimating the importance of scale: You might believe you've planned for scalability, but odds are, your strategies are rife with concealed trouble areas that will haunt you as your company develops. First and foremost, be cautious of process interdependencies. A system is as powerful as its least reliable component. Specifically, any procedure which requires human intervention is going to be a bottleneck for any automated procedures that depends on it, no matter how much hardware you throw at the task. Additionally, cutting corners today is a certain recipe for headaches tomorrow. It may be tempting to piggyback a departmental database onto an underutilized Web server or let an open workstation double as networked storage, but the danger far outweighs the gain. Today's minor project could easily turn into tomorrow's mission-critical source, leaving you with the unenviable job of separating the conjoined twins.

Mismanaging your SaaS strategy: Salesforce.com demonstrated that SaaS (software as a service) has real legs in business computing. In comparison to traditional desktop applications, the on-demand version provides clients a low barrier to entry and practically no upkeep expenses. Little wonder, then, a growing number of software vendors have started offering hosted products in several software categories. If you haven't at least considered SaaS choices, you're doing your business a disservice. An excessive amount of SaaS, on the other hand, can become problematic. Hosted services don't interoperate as well as desktop software, and the level of customization offered by SaaS vendors varies. Bear in mind, SaaS is merely a business model - it's not really a deal if the program itself is immature.

Not profiling your code: Relative performance is a continuing debate among developers. Can code written for a single platform or language run in addition to equivalent code written for a different? Here, software development dovetails with carpentry, since it is frequently the poor craftsman who blames his tools. For every program that suffers due to an inherent flaw in the language, countless others have been rife with poorly designed algorithms, inefficient storage requirements, along with other programmer-created speed lumps. Locating these problem spots is the goal of code profiling, and that is what makes it so essential. Until you've identified the weakest parts of your own code, any effort to optimize it will be fruitless. Perhaps the issue is not your fault after all.

Failing to virtualize: If you are not taking advantage of virtualization, you are just making things harder on yourself. Stacking many VMs onto a single physical machine pushes up system usage, providing you with a greater return on your own hardware investments. Virtualization can also make it easy to provision and de-provision new systems and can be used to make secure sandbox environments for testing new software and OS configurations. Some sellers may tell you that their wares can't be installed in a virtualized environment. If that is true, tell them bye-bye. This is one technology that is too good to pass up.

Putting too much faith in one vendor: It's easy to see why some businesses keep going back to the same vendor again to fulfill all manner of IT needs. Large IT vendors love to provide integrated solutions, and a support contract that promises "one throat to choke" will always be attractive to overworked admins. Keep in mind that if the contract has you relying on immature products which are outside your vendor's core expertise, nevertheless, you could be the one who ends up gasping for breath. Rarely is each entry in an enterprise IT product lineup equal and getting roped into a subpar solution is a mistake that can have long-term repercussions. While providing preferential consideration to present vendor partners makes good business sense, keep in mind that there's nothing wrong with declining when the best-of-breed lies elsewhere.

Plowing ahead with plagued projects: Learn to recognize signs of problems and act decisively. A job can fail for a thousand different reasons but continuing to put money into a failed initiative is only going to compound your missteps. As an example, the Federal Bureau of Investigation wasted four decades and over $100 million on its own Virtual Case File (VCF) electronic record-keeping system, despite repeated warnings from insiders that the job had been dangerously off-track. When the FBI finally pulled the plug in 2005, VCF was still nowhere close to completion. Don't let this be you. Have an exit plan prepared for each job and make certain that you can put it in motion prior to making a false start which becomes a real IT disaster.

Not planning for peak power: Sustainable IT is not just about saving the planet. Additionally, it is superior resource planning. When electricity prices spiral out of control, they threaten business agility and restrict development. Don't wait for your datacenter to achieve capacity to get started looking for ways to lessen your overall power consumption. From CPUs to storage devices, memory to monitors, energy efficiency must be a key consideration for all new hardware purchases. And don't limit your search to hardware alone; software alternatives such as virtualization and SaaS will help consolidate servers and lessen your energy footprint even further. The outcome will not only be a sustainable planet, but a more sustainable venture.

Setting unrealistic project timetables: When planning IT projects, occasionally your own confidence and enthusiasm may be your undoing. An early, optimistic time estimate can quickly morph into a hard deliverable while your back is turned. Because of this, always leave ample time to complete project objectives, even if they seem simple from the beginning. It is always much better to over deliver compared to overcommit. Flexibility will generally be the key to project success. Be sure to identify potential risk areas long before the deadlines are set in stone, especially if you're working with external vendors. By setting expectations at a realistic level throughout the project lifecycle, you can avoid the trap of being made to present incomplete features as deadlines loom.

.

Ch. 9 Common Causes of IT Disasters

Odds are, sooner or later, you will experience an IT tragedy where information is lost or corrupted. The reason may be intended malice, user error, or an environmental variable, but no matter what, the final result is going to be the same: Critical business data might be gone permanently.

Causes of IT disasters are all around us at all times. Being aware of these potential causes can help you build a disaster recovery plan and prevent losing money, time, and clients in case of disaster. Knowing the causes of IT disasters can also help you produce a convincing case to management to get the backup technologies you need.

Here are five causes of IT disasters that businesses tend to overlook:

Hardware and equipment failure: Failure of a hard drive or drives in a server would be the most obvious example for hardware failure. But things such as a failed hard drive controller can also cause corrupt data to be written to a fully operational drive.

Environmental catastrophes: IT disasters may be caused

by major inclement weather events such as flooding, but they may also be due to fire, structural, or equipment failures within a workplace environment. While it may seem obvious that a water heater does not belong close to a host, you may not be in control of what is in the office above the area where a server is found. A water leak in an adjacent wall or area can make a flood condition, which in turn could ruin sensitive computer equipment.

Viruses and other infections: A virus can infect or delete data that is critical. It can be even worse if the lesser-known ransomware is the culprit, like the Cryptolocker virus. An infected machine that stays connected to the system will systematically encrypt all network files it has access to, rendering them useless. The worst part of infections like this is that the files seem to be intact if they aren't opened, so it might take months or weeks to realize that the damage has happened. Having been engaged in many Cryptolocker information recoveries, I can speak to the severity of these incidents. All files will need to be reviewed to ascertain which are infected, and with no proper backup scheme, a great amount of data will be lost.

Malicious intent: The obvious perpetrator here is a hacker or external criminal effort to gain access and cause damage. But sometimes the damage may be caused by internal forces. Ill-intentioned workers can cause IT disasters. A disgruntled worker with the ideal degree of access can easily delete large amounts of data very quickly. And regrettably, you may not realize the amount of the harm done until after the employee is no longer with your company.

Human error or accidental data destruction: I refer to the situation as destruction because it isn't always intentional deletion. A worker may delete a file by mistake or may save a brand-new version of a document over an existing one, without thinking about the consequences of doing this. Even worse, a worker may create a new file with the same name as an existing one rather than heed the overwrite warning when saving.

Safeguards are in place to stop record overwrites, but they are rather easy to unintentionally bypass. In my experience, most users don't carefully read dialog boxes. In fact, when presented with a dialogue box during a document save operate, most users may click anything just to make the box go away so they could shut down and depart for the afternoon.

Ch. 10 Disaster Recovery Planning

Business continuity management policy

Many organizations will have a business continuity management coverage for ensuring that the company can recover from a badly disruptive incident. An effective policy must clearly specify the roles and responsibilities for those responsible for its oversight and implementation along with the minimal requirements for compliance, including levels of IT resilience to disruption and disaster recovery skills. A nicely designed and well-defined policy will be supported by tested and effective procedures and arrangements in place to permit the organization to react to, proceed through, and continue to operate after any event that may severely impair its ability to provide the normal level of support to its clients and stakeholders.

These procedures and arrangements would be the cornerstone of the company's IT resilience.

IT resilience

IT resilience is defined as an organization's ability to keep acceptable service levels throughout, and beyond, severe disruptions to its critical procedures as well as the IT systems which support them. By focusing on the areas of awareness, protection, discovery, planning, recovery, review, and improvement, an organization will minimize the possible effect of disruptions to its IT support which, in today's highly competitive business environment that most of us work in, can be extremely expensive, possibly to the point of complete failure.

These areas are key to effective IT resilience. None can be obtained in isolation - they overlap at some point in the overall process.

Awareness

Awareness is getting the knowledge of what are the normal business needs of operational functionality, dependencies that might exist, the criticality of IT system components, and the minimum acceptable operational levels.

There also has to be an awareness of the recovery needs concerning time, system capacity, and performance in case of severe disruption to, or failure of, IT systems supporting the business procedures. These should be identified through an effective business impact assessment (BIA).

Protection

Protection is more than having physical and system access controls. In addition, it can mean reducing the risk of system failure, e.g. removing single points of failure (SPoF) with load balancing servers, redundant systems, or components. Potential exposures to systems deemed to be critical to business processes should be identified and addressed.

Discovery

Discovery means the quicker the IT team knows that a system was disrupted, the earlier they can resolve the problem. The use of effective means of alarms of issues which enable the IT team to comprehend and address issues before they lead to severe disruption.

Preparedness

Preparedness means having detailed plans for addressing the effects of a disturbance, such as having seamless failover of systems and components, allowing essential business processes to continue to operate with no, or an acceptable minimum, disruption of service.

Recovery

This will only be achieved by having an effective and tested recovery plan with minimal and acceptable data loss following an event causing disruption or failure. Operations return to business as normal levels within defined timescales and with recovery focuses on returning providers.

Review

Review is necessary to each IT resilience program and contains post-incident reviews to identify the root causes of disruptions. It is a continual process which aims to enable the IT team and the business to understand potential problems and to assess and implement preventative actions to remove, or mitigate, the danger of the disruption.

Improvement

Improvement is the procedure of accepting the knowledge obtained from all of the above and taking steps to improve systems and increase resilience, and to continuously enhance disaster recovery and business continuity programs. It needs to be noted here that most, if not all, the data needed for the above to be achieved successfully will probably come from effective business impact assessment/analysis and hazard evaluation.

IT resilience and DR considerations

The ISO/IEC 27031:2011 standard recommends six main categories to be considered when formulating an IT DR (disaster recovery) strategy:

Key competencies and knowledge: What information does one need in order to run the critical IT services? Is it with a service supplier or is it onsite? Or is it a mix of both? How can this information be incorporated into the organization's knowledge bank and be made available in the event of a severely disruptive incident or event requiring IT disaster recovery processes to be activated?

Facilities: What are the standards that installations and infrastructure must meet to minimize the chance of failure or severe disruption and eventual restoration? Where should such facilities be located?

Technology systems: Which systems are most important to the organization's business? Have retrieval requirements been identified, e.g., RTO (recovery time objective), RPO (recovery point objective), or dependencies on other systems?

Data: Has the data required to restore/restart business activities, as well as the timescales within which it must be available been identified? It is to be noted that there may be different RTO and RPO for IT services and information. The recovery or implementation of security controls to secure the information also have to be considered.

Processes: Which processes are in place to deal with an event or disaster, and how can the subjects outlined before, combine to provide the necessary, and defined, business services.

Suppliers: Which service suppliers are crucial to IT continuity, and how do they ensure that they can support the organization's recovery and business continuity requirements? Are these service providers, in turn, dependent upon the successful answers from other third parties, external or internal to their organization?

IT recovery strategies

It makes good business sense to develop and maintain retrieval strategies for IT systems, software, and data. Recovery strategies must address the aforementioned IT disaster recovery considerations and include all of the components which make up each platform, e.g. servers, networks, desktops, laptops, wireless devices, connectivity, and data. Priorities for IT recovery must be consistent with the priorities for recovery of critical business functions and procedures which were identified by an effective BIA (business impact analysis). IT resources necessary to support crucial business functions and procedures also have to be identified.

The recovery period for an IT source should be commensurate with the recovery time objective (RTO) for the business function or procedure that depends on this IT resource. The RTO is the time where a business process has to be restored, and also a stated minimum level of service/performance attained following a disturbance, to prevent unacceptable consequences related to disruption to that service. For each system, this has to be recognized by the business area that is the proprietor or prime user of the system via the BIA. The recovery point objective (RPO) should also be identified through the BIA process. The RPO is the maximum tolerable loss of data from an IT service because of a significant incident. In several system environments, the overall restoration point must be that which returns collaborating systems to some constant, synchronized state.

Additionally, it's always helpful to have recognized the maximum tolerable outage (MTO) which is the maximum period of time that critical systems services may be inaccessible or undeliverable following acute disruption or failure, after which the consequences are unacceptable or intolerable. Without one element, a system may not be in a position to properly support the business operations for which they have been designed.

When developing a recovery strategy, you should develop

it to anticipate a failure, or loss, of one or more of the following system components:

- Physical environment (data center / center building; computer rooms; facilities; utilities)
- Hardware (wireless devices and peripherals; servers; desktop and laptop computers)
- Connectivity (network links; equipment and services)
- Systems software (computer operating systems)
- Middleware (platform services which include web servers and/or application services)
- Enabling software (any central application, such as email)
- Applications (data processing) software
- Data

IT disaster recovery planning (IT DRP)

Disaster recovery planning is the continuing process of planning, developing, executing, and analyzing disaster recovery management procedures and processes to ensure the efficient and effective resumption of critical roles in the event that there is any kind of interruption which might cause severe disruption. A disaster recovery plan could only be effective if system dependencies have been identified and accounted for when creating the arrangement of recovery, establishing recovery time and recovery point objectives and documenting the functions of required personnel.

Roles and responsibilities

Each area within the business, as owners of each system used to support their own processes and services, should ensure that suppliers and hosts of IT services, both external and internal, are conscious of the priority of each platform and its own criticality within each business area's processes.

The company's IT group should ensure that systems provided in house or hosted by IT service providers comply with the organization's resilience and DR capability standards and continue to meet business requirements. IT service providers must be responsible for ensuring that their procedures and processes comply with the customer's requirements and criteria, as stated in contracts and service level agreements (SLAs).

Resilience reviews

To ensure effective implementation of this BCM coverage in terms of IT durability and recovery and continuity of service to the essential level, the company should create a detailed review of what is needed in order to establish the IT business continuity/disaster recovery (BC/DR) resilience of systems behind its company operations, functions, and processes. The reviews should be conducted by a group along with all the necessary professional knowledge, and experience. Reviews should also be done at regular intervals. To guarantee objectivity, this shouldn't be an internal IT function. Reviews must be structured to assess the capability and resilience of IT systems or services supporting business areas or procedures, instead of individual IT systems. Reviews may emphasize potential exposures which, in case of an incident causing severe disruption to IT solutions, may delay or, at a worst-case scenario, avert, retrieval of critical business procedures, services or functions, with potential fiscal and/or reputational damage to the organization. The review process should include evaluation of the procedures, policies and processes associated with preparing for recovery or continuation of technology infrastructure, systems, and software, after an incident that may cause severe disruption to, or collapse of, essential services, from whatever cause. The results of each review must include agreement on corrective actions intended to improve the durability of critical IT systems against acute disruption, with duties for each.

The purpose of corrective action should be to eliminate identified potential risks, or at least reduce them to an acceptable degree to enhance IT resilience. To provide a degree of consistency to the review procedure, the organization must establish a set of criteria and guidelines to which its IT systems must adapt to, and which will also provide advice to system designers and programmers regarding the resilience and DR capabilities that are required. These standards and guidelines will apply to the review of the durability and recovery capability of critical IT infrastructure, applications and systems, and other IT services which are deemed essential to the business. They need to not only apply to IT services that may be operated in house but also ones supplied by approved and contracted third parties.

Why standards are guidelines?

In simple terms, guidelines and standards provide a means to achieve order in a given context. They specify the standards against which the resilience of IT systems supporting business processes and purposes can be reviewed with consistency. At a large and complex business, criteria can address, by way of example, the requirement for interconnection and interoperability, particularly where there's a mixture of equipment and solutions. Effective usage of well thought out criteria provides a solid base upon which to develop new, and improve existing, techniques, and helps you to increase consumer confidence.

What is the difference between a standard and a guideline?

Standards, in this context, are the standards against which, when examined, a system has to be compliant to be considered to be resilient. Guidelines are intended to provide information about the degree of information which are required to be accessible to assess the amount of resilience.
To answer the question, it's good to think in terms of above and below the line:

A **standard** is a must have/must do item and is over the line. Requirements will be stated using terms such as must, will, and shall. E.g. the organization has to have an IT disaster recovery plan that is part of, or feeds right into, the overall business continuity plan procedure. There are no gray areas for criteria; if something isn't as defined in the standard then it's deemed to be non-compliant for its IT DR resilience review purposes.

A **guideline** provides a degree of flexibility in compliance and is considered below the line. The requirements should be stated using such terms as should, may, and could. E.g. the following areas should be considered in the BIA (business impact analysis) review along with details.

This is not to say that guidelines can or should be ignored. These are just advisory statements and non-compliance or non-inclusion must be justified when a review or audit is carried out.

What are the recommended standards and guidelines?

The following list can be considered the minimum needed for inclusion in any organization's IT resilience and DR standards and guidelines.

IT disaster recovery
- IT disaster recovery plan
- System criticality and recovery objectives
- Testing and Review
- IT disaster recovery plan content
- IT service providers: disaster recovery plan information
- New systems

Business impact assessment
- Business impact assessment evidence
- Business area objectives/priorities
- Information Required
- Review
- IT systems planning

Ch. 11 Creating a DR Plan

Disaster Recovery in the IT Management Context

In IT, a crisis is any unexpected problem that results in a slowdown, interruption or failure in an integral system or community. It was mentioned in prior chapters that no matter the cause, service outages, connectivity failures, data loss, and associated technical problems can disrupt company operations, resulting in lost revenues, increased costs, customer service issues, and lowered office productivity. IT disaster recovery planning approaches have to be created to respond to these diverse truths and perceptions. Because of this, a little bit more is needed when creating a DR plan.

To this end, these plans must address three fundamental needs:

Prevention - to prevent and minimize tragedy frequency and occurrence. Anticipation - to identify probable disasters and relevant consequences. And mitigation - to take actions for handling disasters to lessen negative effect.

Fundamental Planning Goals and Objectives

There is not any doubt that disaster recovery preparation can provide many advantages to a business enterprise. As soon as you admit the value of technology to your own organization, you must also look at the related impacts if and when this technology becomes temporarily inaccessible, or totally inaccessible.

Your Willingness and Ability to address these Problems can offer several key operational benefits:

- To decrease the negative impact of any disaster
- To conserve time and money in the recovery process in the event of a catastrophe
- To protect technology assets owned by a company, maximizing ROI
- To minimize regulatory or legal obligations
- To advertise systems and IT service quality, security, and reliability
- To promote the value of technology and related IT services in your organization
- To promote management consciousness, and to set realistic expectations about the demand for systems management tools and resources

Learn to Fast Track

If it comes to handling issues, you need more than a single approach to become consistently reliable. The way that you manage when all conditions are good, isn't the same way you manage when time is running short, resources are stretched too thin and people aren't working together. That is what fast tracking is for.

Disaster Recovery Planning in Practice

In the IT management circles, there are lots of amounts to defining "disaster" and numerous options to address each degree.

To make things easier, the extensive perspective of disaster recovery can be simplified into 3 main preparation categories - prevention, reduction, and anticipation.

Prevention: Avoiding Disaster Events to the Extent Possible

The objective of preventative disaster recovery planning is to ensure that all key systems are as safe and reliable as possible, so as to reduce the frequency or likelihood of technology associated disasters. Since natural disasters usually lie beyond our sphere of influence, prevention most frequently applies to systems issues and human errors, to include physical hardware failures, software bugs, setup errors and omissions, and acts of malicious intent (virus attacks, security offenses, data corruption, etc.). Utilizing the right set of techniques and tools, it's possible to reevaluate both the incidence and related harm from any and all of these kinds of disasters.

Anticipation: Planning for the Most Likely Events

Anticipation strategies revolve round assumptions and the ability to foresee possible disasters, so as to identify possible consequences and appropriate responses. Without a crystal ball, contingency planning can be a challenging process. It involves knowledge and cautious evaluation.

Knowledge comes from experience, data, and an understanding of which systems you need, how they're configured, and what type of issues or failures are likely to occur. And the related analysis entails a careful balancing of circumstances and consequences.

Mitigation: Get Ready to React and Recover

Mitigation is about reaction, recovery, and the capability to respond when and if a disaster happens. Accepting that specific disasters are possible, and perhaps inevitable, the aim of any mitigation strategy is to minimize adverse impact.

- Maintain current technical documentation to facilitate recovery if a problem occurs
- Conduct regular tests of your disaster recovery plans and strategies
- Maintain loaner equipment available for instant usage
- Create normal back-ups of software, hardware, and data configurations
- Maintain an alternative workplace program to allow designated employees to work from home or other places
- Identify standalone or manual operating procedures in case of a prolonged outage

Work together with other corresponding emergency, security, and employee safety programs and policies when you're coordinating your IT disaster recovery plans.

Ch. 12 Expert Tips and Tricks

Let's just summarize some of what was mentioned in the book in order to reiterate some of the easiest tips and tricks to keep in mind when trying to prevent IT disasters.

Patch all third-party applications (I.E Java and Chrome). These third-party programs are normally so vulnerable you could compromise your workstation just by visiting an infected website or link. If you don't know who sent you an email do not click on the links or open the attachments. Since so many people have vulnerable workstations, emails continue to be a very successful way to get malware installed, or to trick users into divulging information. Confirm your privacy settings on mobile devices and social media. Be sure you're not over-sharing information with the entire world that could possibly be used against you.

You wouldn't want to have your personal pictures and information stolen through a malicious email. Keep in mind that you can't lose what you do not have. Think twice before producing anything electronic as malicious email is increasingly common and is enormously effective. You should randomly generate passwords (bar the ones you really need to recall) and use a password manager for everything! A fantastic password manager like 1Password or Keypass. Use multi-step or 2 -actor everywhere.

Always be suspicious - Online or email scams are no longer identifiable by poor grammar and spelling mistakes. Whenever you see advertisements or emails claiming to offer you a free iPhone or iPad, ask yourself if it can occur while walking down the road. System updates - make sure you have the newest version of all installed applications. Although Java or PDF software is commonly targeted, only a few actually take the time to install the latest security updates; Run security software - A current security solution will keep your PC infection-free, as long as you follow a minimum of best practices for internet browsing and file downloading.

Never use the same password twice. As we register for ever more accounts and solutions it becomes extremely tempting to reuse the same password over and over again. However, that can be extremely risky behavior. If your login credentials have been ever caught by a hacker - and together with the amount of data breaches in the news each week it's a case of when, not if the attacker is going to have inadvertently gained access to a whole digital world. When developing a large number of complicated and difficult to guess passwords is a challenge contemplate using a password manager that can save all your passwords for you, leaving you with only a single master password to recall.

Whether you're at home or at work, chances are, you'll receive emails from time to time that are not quite what they seem. Cyber criminals often create convincing emails that seem to come from bank, credit card business, along with other popular sites that hold monetary or other sensitive data. Contained within will be hyperlinks to copycat sites under the bad guys' control which can steal your private data - and perhaps your money too - if you visit them and put in your username and password. We are living in a digital era where we could download just about anything we want to see, listen to, or use and also have access to it almost instantly.

While there are hundreds of legitimate websites from which digital content can be downloaded, you can find tens of thousands more that offer bogus, and dangerous content, filled with malware designed to steal your own financial and other personal info. Is the website well-known? Have any of your friends used the site without incident or unexpected surprises? Is it actually the site you think it is instead of a clone? (Check your browser for a padlock or a URL starting with https:// to get some certainty and do not ever click on a download link sent to you via email).

After more than 20 years working with IT security, it appears to me that lots of individuals still expect to find a 100 percent alternative for all the security issues that plague us and are furious when a simple solution doesn't meet their expectations. Unfortunately, vendor marketing isn't great at anticipation management, often offering simplistic solutions to complicated issues, single solutions which should render all other products obsolete. In reality, the marketing of the idea that single-layer/single-solution security is sufficient isn't just obsolete (if it was ever valid, which I really don't think it ever was), but reckless. I often read that solution X makes passwords outdated. Password methodology has plenty of problems, but the best way to boost authentication isn't simply to replace one (faulty) method with the latest method du jour and expect it to be more reliable.

Many social networking sites now permit you to strengthen password authentication with one secondary authentication system, such as Facebook's Login Approvals, that uses a token (security code) sent to a phone by SMS or its authenticator program. I truly hope that most people today know that viruses are not the only security threat they will need to be worried about. Frequently, all that most users do is install an (often free) anti-virus software. Provided that it is a genuine security program rather than any sort of malicious malware, you still should have additional protections. But keep in mind that there is nothing sufficient to give complete protection.

If you can't bear to invest in security software (preferably an enterprise level security package), then look into the prospect of strengthening your complimentary anti-virus along with other free but genuine, reliable security software such as a browser sandbox. You are a security layer. Having argued (convincingly, I expect) to get multi-layering, on the grounds that where one strategy fails, another might triumph, I will mention a safety layer that often gets overlooked: you personally.

Many sorts of threats rely on social engineering, psychologically manipulating a victim into doing something which will enable the attacker to achieve his aims. I can't teach immunity to complex social engineering tactics in a paragraph -- and even hardened security researchers can be duped occasionally - but if it's possible try to maintain a fair level of skepticism and remember that successful social engineering may use the carrot or the stick (or both). By doing so you can save yourself a great deal of grief. Above all, do not fall into the trap of thinking that security software or your favorite operating system will help save you from needing to make sensible decisions about what links and attachments you open.

Think twice and always be critical when opening attachments from e-mails or documents downloaded from the Internet. Ask yourself whether you trust the source and why you would want to download it at the first place. Update your programs and applications. Patch your software when new security patches are released.

Back up everything - not only your computer but also your phone and your tablet. Back up your systems so that you can restore them even if the building burns down.

Exploits are a developing infection vector for individuals and companies alike right now. Make sure you run technical anti-exploit technology and use a browser that's less likely to be vulnerable to exploits. Keep your daily applications, such as browsers, Java, and PDF readers, up to date at all times. Patch fast.

Layered security is important! Run dedicated anti-malware along with your traditional anti-virus solution.

Keep all of your applications up-to-date, your Windows operating system as well as the 3rd party software. Online hackers always target applications vulnerabilities and security exploits present in unpatched software, so be sure you have them all protected with the latest security patches.

Use very complicated passwords and 2-step verification. Do not use your dog's name or any easy to guess password. Think of yourself as a target for hackers when using your computer and think about what it is you do. In today's security landscape, we will need to admit that sensitive data and private data is under threat from cyber-criminals. At the same time, use common sense and be sure that you don't access strange looking sites or respond to phishing e-mails.

Nothing is free of charge. This is particularly true for programs or software. Free usually means that you will have to provide them access to your private information. Third party information collectors are as great a threat to privacy as police surveillance. Learn who's collecting your personal or company information, how they intend to utilize it, for how long, and whether they will share what they collect from you.

Ch. 13 Windows File Extensions

Most people today understand that .exe documents are potentially dangerous, but that isn't the only file extension to beware of on Windows. There are a variety of other potentially dangerous file extensions - more than you may be aware of. It is important to understand which file extensions are possibly dangerous when determining if a document attached to an email or downloaded from the internet is safe to open. Even screen saver documents can be dangerous on Windows. When you experience one of those files, you should take additional care to make sure you are protected. Scan with your preferred anti-virus solution, or perhaps upload it into a service such as "VirusTotal" to ensure that there are no viruses or malware.

Evidently, you should always have your antivirus software running, active, and shielding you in the background - but knowing more about some rare file extensions may be useful in preventing something bad from happening.

Why is a file extension potentially dangerous? These file extensions are potentially harmful because they can contain code or execute arbitrary commands. An .exe file is potentially dangerous since it is a program that can do anything (within the limits of Windows' User Account Control feature). Media files -- such as .JPEG pictures and .MP3 music documents -- aren't dangerous because they can't contain code. (There are some cases where a maliciously crafted image or other media file can exploit a vulnerability in a viewer application, but these issues are infrequent and are patched fast.) With that in mind, it is important to know precisely what kinds of files can contain scripts, code, and other possibly dangerous items.

Programs:

.EXE – The most common executable program file. Most Windows applications are .exe files.

.PIF – An information file for programs running MS-DOS. PIF files don't normally have any executable code but if they do, Windows will treat them the same as .EXE files.

.APPLICATION – An installer that comes with Microsoft's Click Once technology.

.GADGET – For the Windows desktop gadget technology which was introduced in Windows Vista.

.MSI – An installer file from Microsoft. These install applications on your computer the same way that .exe files do.

.MSP – A Windows patch. Used to patch programs deployed with .MSI files.

.COM – The first kind of program which was used by MS-DOS.

.SCR – A screen saver by Windows. It is sometimes possible for Windows screen savers to contain executable code.

.HTA – A type of HTML application that is not usually run in browsers.

.CPL – A Control Panel file. All of the applications and systems in the Windows Control Panel are .CPL files.

.MSC – Stands for Microsoft Management Console file. The group policy editor and the disk management tool are both examples of

.MSC files.

.JAR – These files are executable Java code. .JAR files will be run like any other program if the Java runtime is installed.

Scripts:

.BAT – A batch file. These files have a list of commands for the computer to run.

.CMD – Another batch file and similar to .BAT. This came with Windows NT.

.VB, .VBS – A VBScript file. It's an executable if it's run.

.VBE – An encrypted VBScript file. Similar to a VBScript file, but you can't tell what it will do if it's run.

.JS – A JavaScript file. .JS files are often used by webpages and are usually safe if run in Web browsers. However, be careful because Windows will run .JS files outside the browser as well.

.JSE – An encrypted JavaScript file.

.WS, .WSF – A script file for Windows.

.WSC, .WSH – These control files stand for Windows Script Component and Windows Script Host. They are usually used together with other script files.

.PS1, .PS1XML, .PS2, .PS2XML, .PSC1, .PSC2 – Different Windows PowerShell scripts. They always run the commands in the order stated.

.MSH, .MSH1, .MSH2, .MSHXML, .MSH1XML, .MSH2XML – Before PowerShell, there were Monad script files. Later, they were renamed PowerShell.

Shortcuts:

.SCF – A command file for Windows Explorer. It's possible to pass unwanted commands to Windows Explorer.

.LNK – A shortcut to a program on your computer. It's possible to contain commands which can do almost anything to a program - even delete it.

.INF – A text file used by AutoRun. This file could launch dangerous applications.

Other:
.REG – Windows registry files. These files add or remove entries in the registry. A dangerous .REG file could cause applications, or even the operating system, to stop functioning.
.DOC, .XLS, .PPT – Microsoft Office documents. Word, Excel, and Powerpoint. It can contain dangerous macro code.
.DOCM, .DOTM, .XLSM, .XLTM, .XLAM, .PPTM, .POTM, .PPAM, .PPSM, .SLDM – These file extensions were introduced in Office 2007. The M at the end stands for Macros. Notice that a .DOCX file doesn't contain any macros, while a .DOCM file may.

This is not an exhaustive list. There are different types of file extensions - such as .PDF - which have had a string of security issues. However, for most of the file types above, there's just no avoiding them. They exist to run random code or commands on your computer. As if the amount of potentially dangerous file extensions to keep track of was not enough, A vulnerability in Windows allows malicious individuals to disguise apps with file extensions that are bogus.

Conclusion

Cybersecurity is one of the most important aspects of the fast-paced growing digital world and I would argue that it's only going to become more important as time goes on. The threats of it are hard to deny, so it is crucial to learn how to defend from them and teach others how to do it too. You don't have to become a cybersecurity expert. Even a basic understanding of cybersecurity will put you far ahead of the pack and will prevent you and your organization from being an easy target. Don't forget these important security measures:

- Install and regularly update antivirus software for every computer used in business, home, or other places. Do a little research and find the best protection provider on the internet and don't buy the cheapest software.
- Protect your internet connection by using a firewall.
- Make backup copies for important data and keep them safe.
- Train employees or family members about cyber security and its' principles.
- Regularly change passwords and use strong ones. A strong password contains lower-case, capital letters and numbers. It is recommended to not make it a word, just a random combination.
- Regularly update computer software and operating systems.
- Secure the network.

REFERENCES

Chapter 1

Mitnick Security "Kevin Mitnick, The Most Famous Hacker in History" by Tamtata on March 14, 2016. Available at https://www.mitnicksecurity.com/S=0/site/news_item/kevin-mitnick-the-most-famous -hacker-in-history

Mitnick Security. "About Kevin Mitnick; CEO, Team Leader and Chief White Hat Hacker". Available at https://www.mitnicksecurity.com/S=0/about/kevin-mitnick-worlds-most-famous-hacker-biography

Tom's Hardware. "The Fifteen Greatest Hacking Exploits" by Nicolas Aguila. Available at http://www.tomshardware.com/reviews/fifteen-greatest-hacking-exploits,1790-11.html

Wikipedia. "Kevin Mitnick" on July 25, 2016. Available at https://en.wikipedia.org/wiki/Kevin_Mitnick

Wired. "Catching Kevin" on February 1, 1996. Available at http://www.wired.com/1996/02/catching/

CNN. "I hacked into a nuclear facility in the '80s. You're welcome." By Timothy Winslow on May 3, 2016. Available at http://edition.cnn.com/2015/03/11/tech/computer-hacker-essay-414s/

Unhinged reviews. "The 414s: The Original Teenage Hackers— Documentary" on November 13, 2015. Available at http://www.unhingedreviews.com /movies/the-414s-the-original-teenage-hackers-documentary-unhinged

Wikipedia. "The 414s" on July 5, 2016. Available at https://en.wikipedia.org/wiki/The_414s

Black Hole. "The Legion of Doom" July 10, 2012. Available at http://blackhat-noob.blogspot.com.eg/2012/07/legion-ofdoom.html

Wikipedia. "Legion of Doom" on July 11, 2016. Available at https://en.wikipedia.org/wiki/Legion_of_Doom_(hacking)

Limn. "The Morris Worm." Christopher Kelty. Available at http://limn.it/the-morris-worm/

Wikipedia. "Morris Worm." March 6, 2016. Available at https://en.wikipedia.org/wiki/Morris_worm

https://www.mitnicksecurity.com/site/news_item/kevin-mitnick-the-most-famous-hacker-in-history

Chapter 2

Wikipedia. "Nahshon Even-Chiam" on August 5, 2016. Available at https://en.wikipedia.org/wiki/Nahshon_Even-Chaim

The New York Times. "Computer Savvy, With an Attitude; Young Working-Class Hackers Accused of High-Tech Crime" by Mary B. W. Tabor with Anthony Ramirez on July 23, 1992. Available at http://www.nytimes.com/1992/07/23/nyregion/computer-savvy-with-attitude-young-working-class-hackers-accused-high-tech-crime.html?pagewanted=all

Wikipedia. "Masters of Deception" on April 19, 2016. Available at https://en.wikipedia.org/wiki/Masters_of_Deception

Wikipedia. "Operation Sundevil" on June 22, 2016. Available at https://en.wikipedia.org/wiki/Operation_Sundevil#cite_note-Sterling2-5

Motherhood. "A Brief Look Back at One of Canada's Most Notorious Hacker Pranks" by Adam Jackson on December 9, 2014. Available at http://motherboard.vice.com/read/a-brief-look-back-at-one-of-canadas-most-notorious-hacker-pranks https://en.wikipedia.org/wiki/Nahshon_Even-Chaim

https://www.washingtonpost.com/archive/business/1992/07/09/5-indicted-in-computer-infiltration/58bebef5d0684ef28f6af0512788e55b/?utm_term=.2e94 a8af4c78

https://static.anarchivism.org/cyberpunkreviewarchive/www.cyber punkreview.com/2012/03/index.html

Chapter 3
SANS Institute InfoSec Reading Room. "The Changing Face of Distributed
Denial of Service Mitigation," 2001. Available at https://www.sans.org /reading-room/whitepapers/threats/changing-face-distributed-denial -service-mitigation-462

Wikipedia. "Mafiaboy" March 14, 2016. Available at https://en.wikipedia.org/wiki/MafiaBoy

McAfee White Paper by Dmitri Alperovitch, Vice President,

Threat Research, McAfee. Available at http://www.mcafee.com/us/resources/white-papers/wp-operation-shady-rat.pdf

"Operation Shady RAT Pointing the Way," Paul Rubens, eSecurity Planet, August 29, 2011. Available at http://www.esecurityplanet.com/hackers/operation-shady-rat-pointing-the-way.html

"Operations Shady Rat—Unprecedented Cyber-espionage Campaign and Intellectual-Property Bonanza," Michael Joseph Gross, *Vanity Fair*, August 2, 2011. Available at http://www.vanityfair.com/news/2011/09/operation-shady-rat-201109

"Operation Shady Rat—What It Really Means, and What You Can Learn From IT?" TAL Global, August 4, 2011. Available at http://talglobal.com/operation-shady-rat-what-it-really-means-and-what-you-can-learn-from-it/

"7 Lessons: Surviving A Zero-Day Attack," John Foley, September 19, 2011.
Available at http://www.darkreading.com/attacks-and-breaches/7-lessons-surviving-a-zero-day-attack/d/d-id/1100226?

Wikipedia. "Operation Shady RAT" September 27, 2015. Available at https://en.wikipedia.org/wiki/Operation_Shady_RAT

Symantec. "Trojan.Zbot" by Ben Nahorney and Nicolas Falliere. Available at https://www.symantec.com/security_response/writeup.jsp?docid=2010-011016-3514-99

Wikipedia. "Zeus (malware)" on May 22, 2016. Available at

https://en.wikipedia.org/wiki/Zeus_%28malware%29

https://www.justice.gov/opa/pr/international-cybercriminal-extradited-thailand-united-states

http://www.hstoday.us/channels/dhs/single-article-page/cyber-experts-warn-airlines-should-be-in-a-cyber-panic-over-potential-vulnerabilities.html

Chapter 4
"Stuxnet Five Years Later: Did We Learn the Right Lesson?" Andrew Ginter, April 2, 2015. Available at http://www.darkreading.com/risk/stuxnet-five-years-later-did-we-learn-the-right-lesson/a/d-id/1319740

Wikipedia. "Stuxnet." March 10, 2016. Available at https://en.wikipedia.org/wiki/Stuxnet

CloudFlare. "Inside Shellshock: How Hackers are Using it to Exploit Systems" by John Graham-Cumming on September 30, 2014. Available at https://blog.cloudflare.com/inside-shellshock/

Computer Weekly. "Security Think Tank: Use Vulnerability Management for Shellshock" by Vladimir Jirasek on November 2014. Available at http://www.computerweekly.com/opinion/Security-Think-Tank-Use-vulnerability-management-triage-processes-to-deal-with-Shellshock.

Secure Banking Solutions. "Shellshock and Lessons Learned from Heartbleed" by Cody Delzer. Available at https://www.protectmybank .com /shellshock-lessons-learned-heartbleed/

TrendMicro. "Bash Vulnerability Leads to Shellshock: What It Is, How It Affects You." Available at http://blog.trendmicro.com/trendlabs-security-intelligence/shell-attack-on-your-server-bash-bug-cve-2014-7169-and-cve-2014-6271/

Wikipedia. "Shellshock (software bug)" on May 10, 2016. Available at https://en.wikipedia.org/wiki/Shellshock_%28software_bug%29

CNBC. "HSBC Cyberattack Brings Internet Banking to Its Knees." Emma Dunkley, January 29, 2016. Available at http://www.cnbc.com/2016/01/29/hsbc-cyber-attack-brings-Internet-banking-down.html

The Guardian. "HSBC Suffers Online Banking Cyberattack." Hilary Osborne, January 29, 2016. Available at http://www.theguardian.com/money/2016/jan/29/hsbc-online-banking-cyber-attack

Forbes. "Cybersecurity Lessons Learned from 'Panama Papers' Breach" by Jason Bloombery on April 21, 2016. Available at http://www.forbes.com/sites/jasonbloomberg/2016/04/21/cybersecurity-lessons-learned-from-panama-papers-breach/#15db36c24f7a

Wikipedia. "Panama Papers," last updated on July 17, 2016. Available at https://en.wikipedia.org/wiki/Panama_Papers

https://en.wikipedia.org/wiki/Stuxnet

https://embeddedsw.net/doc/Embeddedsw_news_Stuxnet_white_paper.html

http://ware.zintegra.com/tag/israel/

https://en.wikipedia.org/wiki/Shellshock_%28software_bug%29

https://www.theguardian.com/money/2016/jan/29/hsbc-online-banking-cyber-attack

https://www.ft.com/content/851f37c6-c68c-11e5-b3b1-7b2481276e45

http://www.huffingtonpost.co.uk/entry/panama-papers whistleblower_uk_572ccf98e4b05c31e571ffcd

https://www.forbes.com/sites/jasonbloomberg/2016/04/21/cyberse curity-lessons-learned-from-panama-papers-breach/#121a4e292003

https://www.forbes.com/sites/jasonbloomberg/2016/04/21/cyberse curity-lessons-learned-from-panama-papersbreach/#6016eb7e2003

https://www.forbes.com/sites/jasonbloomberg/2016/04/21/cyberse curity-lessons-learned-from-panama-papers-breach/#4faab9892003

https://www.scmagazineuk.com/updated-panama-papers-who-let-the-docs-out/article/531685/

Chapter 7
https://www.ic3.gov/media/2019/190910.aspx#fn1

https://www.fbi.gov/news/stories/2019-internet-crime-report-released-021120

https://enterprise.verizon.com/resources/reports/2020-data-breach-investigations-report.pdf

MATT OLIVIER

ABOUT THE AUTHOR

Matt Olivier is an IT professional and educator specializing in computer networks and cyber security.

He has seen and participated in the rapid advancements in computer technology from the early 90's to the present.

Matt is a perpetual student of technology and computers are not only his career, but also his passion.

www.ingramcontent.com/pod-product-compliance
Lightning Source LLC
Chambersburg PA
CBHW071142050326
40690CB00008B/1545